D1034915

MICHAEL LANCASTER

BRITAIN IN VIEW

Colour and the Landscape

Foreword by Richard Gloucester

Quiller Press
London

A Sandtex Book

First published by
Quiller Press, Ltd., 50 Albemarle St.,
London W1X 4BD

First published 1984

ISBN 0 907621 29 5

Jacket design by Alan Keeler
Book design by Tim McPhee

Design and production in association with Book Production Consultants, 47 Norfolk Street, Cambridge

Printed by Toppan International

Cover.
Top left *Cottage in Sussex.*
Top right *Rainbow. Berwickshire.*
Bottom left *Renault Centre. Swindon.*
Bottom right *Church, Southwark, London.*

Back cover
Standing stone, Avebury. (Roger Seijo)

The author

Michael Lancaster, RIBA ALI, is an architect and landscape architect with wide experience of practice both in Britain and overseas. Abroad, he was responsible for the landscape design for Islamabad, the new capital city of Pakistan, while at home he has recently supervised the establishment of the first honours degree course in landscape architecture in London. He is co-editor of the *Oxford Companion to Gardens*, currently in preparation. His long-standing interest in all aspect of environmental design, and in particular, colour, is expressed in this book.

Acknowledgements

The author wishes to thank the many people and organisations who assisted with information and advice in the preparation of this book. These include: Professor A C Hardy, Tom Porter, Dr Nick Pillans, Elizabeth Bryan, Dr Anthony Quiney, Dr Patrick Goode, Garry Philipson, Marian Thompson, Paul Walshe, John Pike, Dr Rex Savidge, Professor Peter Youngman and Marc Wolfe-Cowen. In particular I should like to thank Mr H L Gloag for his considerable sympathetic help with references and advice on the first part of the book, Dame Sylvia Crowe for reading the manuscript and for her advice on aspects of landscape, and Tom Turner and my wife for continuous detailed advice. Needless to say the views expressed are my own.

Also I am indebted to those who went to some lengths to provide illustrations, particularly: Heather Blackett, Biagio Guccione, A C Hardy, John Pike, Marian Thompson, Tom Turner, Roger Seijo and Paul Walshe; also my sons and daughter for photographs and drawings. Unacknowledged illustrations are my own.

It should be noted that coloured inks on the small scale of the page can never precisely reproduce the evanescent colours that are seen in the field; they are only an approximation. Moreover their concentration and close juxtaposition on the page inevitably changes them in our perceptions. They can only be used for guidance. The only way to study applied colour effectively is in the landscape itself.

Michael Lancaster, January 1984

Contents

Foreword

By Richard Gloucester R.I.B.A.

Mechanisation has enabled mankind to recreate the landscape at a rate and at a scale unequalled in the past, both with new roads and motorways, and by building houses, factories and farm buildings. It has also provided their builders with a huge choice of building materials, many of them artificial and thus given them the responsibility for choosing the colours that increasingly come to dominate the landscape.

This is a responsibility that previous generations did not have to make, for they used the local building material, whether stone or brick, and thus automatically perpetuated the architectural harmony found in our ancient villages and towns.

This new and important responsibility arises at a time when research is revealing much more to us about our perception of colour and its effect. The choices can now be made more empirically than in the past.

This book is for all of us who appreciate colour in our surroundings. It clarifies much of the complexity and explains a method for rational decisions based on an educated view of the subject. I hope it will prove useful to those whose decisions affect the countryside and our cities and thus bring greater order to the visual clutter that is so frequently revealed in our changing landscape.

Richard Gloucester

View across Barnes Pond, London.

Introduction

In sunlight a building may appear as a bright target against the background of the landscape: if white, it is seen in strong reflective contrast to the darker green background of vegetation; if red, the reflective value is nearer to that of the green, and we are more conscious of a contrast of hue between the complementary red and green. If the colour of the building is similar but not too close to that of its background – as in the case of a red building set amidst yellow corn or brown ploughland – we see a relationship of similar hues. But if the colours are too closely related, as happens with green buildings in the landscape, we may sense a disturbing ambiguity. As we get closer to such buildings our perception of colour is displaced by our awareness of the material, so that unless the surfaces are painted, we no longer see them as disembodied surfaces of colour. We begin instead to notice the different colours of its various elements – doors and windows for example, and on a smaller scale bricks and mortar, whose colours have been visually mixed.

Colour, which precisely, if not very romantically defined, is light of different wavelengths reflected at different degrees of intensity from the surfaces of the earth and sky (including water droplets, dust, molecules of carbon dioxide and other substances). It varies according to the nature of the light source, the distance from which it is seen, and the texture of the surface from which it is reflected; it varies also in our perceptions. Thus we 'see' trees as green although they may appear as grey or green or blue or black, according to the light of day. By a process known as *colour constancy* we perceive their 'true' or *local colour* as green. Our brain's responses to the colour sensations transmitted by our eyes is highly complex and only now beginning to be understood[1].

Apart from the mobile surfaces of air and water, the surfaces with which we are concerned in environmental terms are of three types: mineral, vegetable, and artificial or applied. The mineral background constitutes the flesh and bones of the landscape – earth and rocks as seen in mountains and sea cliffs, exposed rock faces, mineral workings and fallow land. The latter is becoming rarer as winter crops are encouraged. Mineral colour, either in its natural or processed form, can also be seen in the majority of building materials. It appears on the surfaces of buildings and roads and forms the background colour of our towns. Vegetable colour in the form of grass, hedges, trees and crops, is the background of the countryside. Artificial colour is seen in the colour of paints, plastics and other applied surfaces which do not have an obvious natural place in the scheme of things. In general we may consider the first two categories as reflecting colour which is incidental to their nature as materials (although of great importance). In the third category, that of applied colour, the use becomes more specific and more contrived. There are of course specific uses of all categories: of plants selected – and even bred – for their colour, and of natural building materials carefully selected for their colour.

Until the nineteenth century, when mass production and cheap transport distributed materials to all parts of the country, colour was usually incidental. Natural materials were chosen because they were locally available and seemed appropriate to the area. To a greater or lesser degree, they had an affinity with the landscape from which they were derived. Where colour wash or distemper was used it was usually white or coloured with earth pigments. Woodwork was not generally painted before the eighteenth century, when softwoods were imported to take the place of oak, which was becoming expensive[2]. Then we may assume there was a general consistency in the choice of colours, subject as they were to availability and local tradition. Innovation was usually – although not always – the prerogative[3] of the landlord who could exercise a controlling influence on his domain, individual identity being expressed in small variations in the form, detail and colours of the building.

Industrialisation, mass-production, and democracy have since shifted the balance away from natural materials towards the synthetic. Although the former are still used, and there has been a revival in the use of brick, we have to come to terms with new materials: they are important. Just as we value the old materials for their variety, strength and durability, we value the new for their lightness, flexibility and precision. In order to develop and at the same time conserve what is good from our past we need to find satisfactory ways of integrating the new with the old. Imitation is inappropriate, concealment is ineffectual. As Lewis Mumford has written in relation to the city, we need 'to enrich the future by maintaining in the midst of change visible structural links with the past in all its cultural richness and variety'[4]. This we can achieve by painstaking concern for all apsects of the new: siting, scale, form, detail, texture and colour. Of these colour is a common denominator, the one factor by and through which one understands the world.

Colour is essential to our lives. We acknowledge its importance in our choice of food, of clothing and the objects with which we surround ourselves. We know its capacity to stimulate or to depress; to give atmosphere and identity to a place, and we are familiar with its symbolic use. Now, with our new freedom, we need to learn to see it in environmental terms: to see how our houses, shops, farms, factories, power stations are all linked by the unifying mineral, vegetable and applied colours of our environment.

Britain may be likened to an old but much-loved carpet: the ground colour is the background of hills and rocks, forests and rivers; the pattern the intricate landscape of towns, villages and farms. In some parts it is still beautiful, in others threadbare; some areas are badly darned in the wrong colours, some so intricately stitched as to be a glorious embellishment. As it becomes more threadbare and more patched, we need to look again, in three dimensions, like the eighteenth-century landowners who created so much of our landscape, in order to 'enrich the future'.

To appreciate and use colour, we must first be able to understand something of its nature, and this is the subject of the first part of the book. The second part, the Geography of Colour, surveys the past and present uses of colour, with particular reference to colour in the landscape and buildings in town and country, related to specific areas and regions. The third part deals with the uses of colour in integrating new structures into the landscape of town and country. The final part, Colour Guidelines, offers advice to those of us concerned with the use of colour in the environment.

Rainbow. Most people see only six distinct colours in the rainbow. Newton, relying upon an assistant 'whose eyes for distinguishing colours were more critical than mine', [1] *gave it seven, thus relating it to the seven known planets and the seven notes of the diatonic code. It is caused by low sunlight penetrating drops of water. The light rays are split by refraction and then reflected back to the observer at the rainbow angle of 41–42 degrees. A secondary bow is seen at an angle of 52–54 degrees when the raindrops are large enough to reflect the light rays twice before emerging. It is always fainter than the primary bow because some of the light escapes.*

The nature of colour

Colour, like space, has no substance: it exists only in the mind. Its effects are perceived through the eyes in the light reflected when the rays of the sun, or another source of light, fall upon the innumerable particle surfaces of earth and sky. These light rays, consituting white light, which divides into the spectrum seen in a rainbow, are only a very small part of the total range of electro-magnetic radiation known to be emitted by the sun, including ultra-violet, infra-red, radio and X-rays. The colour effect depends upon their rate of vibration, each spectral colour having its own wavelength, from red (the longest) to violet (the shortest), vibrating almost twice as fast as red[1]. Light is seen through the eye by a highly complex system of rods and cone-shaped cells contained in the retina, the rods collectively being sensitive to light and movement, and the cones being sensitive to colour. When light enters these receptors it sets up a photo–chemical reaction.

The human eye is believed to contain about 100 million rods and about 6 million cones connected to the optic fibres in a highly complex way. As there are only about 1 million of the latter to pass on the information to the brain and visual cortex it is likely that some form of colour coding occurs in the neural tissues of the retina[2]. The rods are arranged around the perimeter of the retina and the cones generally evenly distributed towards the middle. In the small centre of the retina called the fovea the receptors are so tightly packed that they look like rods. Curiously, although this small area is thought to give the best visual detail and colour, it is less sensitive than the more primitive rod regions of the retina. Astronomers 'look off' the fovea when they wish to detect very faint stars to allow the image to fall on a region of the retina rich in sensitive rods[3]. R L Gregory suggests that: 'by moving from the centre of the human retina to its periphery we travel back in evolutionary time; from the most highly organised structure to a primitive eye, which does little more than detect movements of shadows. The very edge of the human retina does not even give a sensation when stimulated by movement. It gives primitive unconscious vision; and directs the highly-developed foveal region to where it is likely to be needed for its high acuity'.[4]

The arrangement of the cones in the middle of the retina and the rods around the edge explains the different between daytime colour vision and that of the night when the rods come fully into play, and colour almost disappears. As the light fades we become more aware of blues because the rods respond more efficiently to the shorter wavelengths in the blue-green region of the spectrum. The cones are most sensitive to yellow light[5]. Birds, fish, reptiles and some insects respond to colour, but only human beings and some of the closely-related apes appear to have highly developed colour vision. Bees have a visual spectrum which extends to ultra-violet, which we cannot see, but they are deficient at the red of the spectrum; it is the ultra-violet and yellow light reflected by red flowers to which they are attracted. Hens are sensitive to some bright colours, but because their eyes contain only a small proportion of rods, they are less sensitive than ours in the dark. In experiments cats have responded to coloured surfaces only above a certain critical size. Most other animals, including dogs and bulls, have only very rudimentary colour vision. It is upon movement, that their survival depends.[6].

Colour is a sensation induced by light (although we can see colour in our dreams), which may be natural in the form of sunlight, moonlight or starlight; or artificial in the form of incandescent filament or fluorescent light. Each has its own characteristics. Natural daylight comprises direct sunlight and reflected skylight. Sunlight has characteristics shared by wick, filament and other point light sources: it highlights surfaces and casts sharp shadows, thereby accentuating form and texture. Skylight on the other hand, is diffused, resembling the light from fluorescent lamps in producing only weak shadows. The proportion of direct sunlight to reflected skylight varies according to the location, the time of day, and the atmospheric conditions. The mist and cloud resulting from high humidity, as well as dust and industrial pollution cause the light to be diffused. The apparent blueness of the sky is thought to be due to the effect of particles of the atmosphere scattering the sunlight. This affects mostly the shorter wavelengths, making the sky appear violet (to which our eyes are not very sensitive) mixed with a quantity of blue, a little green and very small amounts of yellow and red[7]. But the colours are constantly changing. The presence of dust over cities, as well as deserts, dilutes the blue, giving it a whitish quality. A similar effect of blueness can be seen in the smoke of a bonfire against a dark background. Against a light background it looks yellowish.

Typically, the first light of day is grey and shadowless. When the sun rises the long spectral wavelengths of red and orange tint the sky. As the day progresses the shorter wavelengths become predominant, and the colour of the sky appears blue, tending towards white at noon, and then blue again, progressively coloured by yellow, orange and red as the longer-penetrating wavelengths take over towards sunset. Fog has the effect of eliminating shadows and subduing colours, and cloud reduces the penetration of red, orange and yellow wavelengths. But mist and humidity can, by moistening surfaces, have the effect of intensifying colours[8].

Apart from the effects of light and atmosphere, colour depends upon the spectral properties of the materials on which the light is falling. All materials express colour, whether or not they have been deliberately coloured. Textured and matt surfaces reflect diffusely; smooth surfaces reflect directly. Thus varnished material appears more strongly coloured than untreated material, gloss paint appears stronger than matt, and wet surfaces more intense than dry; unless their colour is obscured by light reflected from the surface. When this happens their brightness or light–reflective quality will predominate over their capacity to reflect colour, and they will appear lighter – a familiar problem when displaying pictures.

In terms of physics, objects have no colour. When white light, or sunlight, strikes a surface some is reflected directly; the rest is broken down into its constituent rays which are either absorbed or reflected according to the molecular structure of the material. We describe the surface colour by the colour of these reflected rays. If all the rays are reflected the surface appears white; if all are absorbed it appears black. If most of the rays pass through the material it will appear transparent, but the rays will be slowed by varying degrees according to their wavelengths. This occurs in the case of the rainbow: refraction caused by the water droplets in the atmosphere breaks down the sunlight into the colours of the spectrum. The tendency to absorb and reflect light determines the apparent colour characteristics of the material. A red surface appears so red because it absorbs fewer red rays than other rays of the spectrum. Coloured surfaces throw coloured reflections on to surrounding surfaces. If red is reflected on to white, the white may appear pinkish. If it falls onto a green surface, the latter may appear grey, because red and green tend to neutralise one another. If the red light falls onto a black surface the black is likely to appear brownish. The glossier the surface, the stronger the reflection.

Summer storm. As the sun moves towards the horizon, more and more of the short wavelengths are absorbed by the atmosphere, which transmits mainly long ones. The intense red and yellow light turns everything to gold, transforming objects into the illuminant mode. All colours: greens, reds, browns and greys, are united in the harmony of a single dominant hue, contrasted with the dark blue-grey of the sky.

In studying these changes the Impressionist painters turned their attention to the atmosphere of colour. After 1890 figures almost disappear from Monet's paintings. He stopped travelling and began to concentrate upon series of paintings of individual subjects: haystacks, poplars, Rouen cathedral and the Gare St Lazare. The rural subjects are totally lacking in topographical interest and even the cathedral paintings tell us little about the architecture. He had become absorbed, as Turner had fifty years before, in the changing effects of light and shade to the extent that the subject was of secondary importance. 'For me a landscape does not exist in its own right, since its appearance changes at every moment; but the surrounding atmosphere brings it to life — the air and the light which vary continually. For me, it is only the surrounding atmosphere which gives subjects their true value.' He was attracted by the mists and fogs of London which he painted on several occasions: 'I like London only in the winter; without the fog, London would not be a beautiful city. It is the fog which gives it its marvellous breadth. Its regular, massive blocks become grandiose in this mysterious cloak.'[9] Here he is drawing attention to the apparent difference in scale between buildings seen in direct sunlight with shadows, and seen in diffused light. The difference in colour expression has been described as *'the object mode'* and the *illuminant mode*.[10] In the first the colours are seen as essentially belonging to objects, expressing the characteristics of form and texture which help us to identify them and locate them in space. In the second, the illuminant mode, colours are disembodied, separate from the objects. Monet, like Turner, became preoccupied with the latter: 'what I want to reproduce is what exists between the subject and me.'[11] In attempting to capture these atmospheric effects both painters moved further and further away from 'the real object', becoming absorbed in a world of light. Turner

1

2

3

4

took the whole landscape as his subject. Monet, working largely in his studio in the slow medium of oil paint on several canvases at a time, created a more private world of harmonious colours. He transformed his water garden, originally created simply because he liked gardening, 'into a single decorative theme' enveloping the viewer in a large oval room created for the purpose.[12]

Colour constancy

1–10. *Ten views of the River Thames at Barnes, London, showing different colour effects due to different weather conditions, times of day, and seasons. How do we know that the trees are green when we see them so many different colour?*

1. *Sunshine casts strong shadows, emphasising form and colour. Here the yellowness of the morning sun stresses the yellows and browns of autumn.*

2. *The dark blue-grey of the sky is strongly contrasted with the green which has been yellowed by the morning sun.*

3. *The yellow sky strengthens the greens and makes the tarmac of the road appear yellow.*

4. *Fog eliminates shadows, flattens volumes into shapes, and mutes colours.*

5. *The light is diffused by the typical cloudy summer sky. Cloud at noon tends to suppress the long, warm wavelengths of red and yellow light in favour of the short, cool blue ones, which give a whitish-blue tint to the landscape.*

6. *The purple-blue of the clouds contrasts with the pinkish-red of the sunset, which is reflected on to the clouds and back on to the wall.*

7. *Under the heavy grey cloud the green trees assume a blackish quality.*

8. *The redness of the sky reflected on all things neutralises the green of the trees, making them appear black.*

9. *The light reflected white from the cumulus clouds is highly distractive against the blue sky and the dark green trees.*

10. *The heavily overcast 'snow' sky gives a purplish-blue cast to the light. Contrasts are emphasised by the snow on the ground and the lack of mist.*

5

6

7

8

9

10

Colour description

Considering that we can with the human eye distinguish between several thousand of the millions of colours that can be produced in hues of varying degrees of lightness and intensity, it is surprising that we have so few specific words to describe them. In fact, there are only about a dozen. All other verbal descriptions rely upon qualifying adjectives such as light or dark, linked colour words such as blue-green, names related to materials or objects such as gold, lemon or ivory, or names more loosely associated with places of origin, like magenta and ultra-marine. The terminology, and the acknowledgement and use of the colours has always depended upon the need and availability. The oldest colour terms in every language are words for dark and light, corresponding to black and white. The next oldest word – 'red' – is commonly used to describe a whole range of colours from yellow to brown[1]. Such words would often be used in the restricted sense of applying to particular materials, like the word for green in the Phillipine Hanunoo language which refers to the light-greens, yellows and browns of bamboo[2]. Desert dwellers, as might be expected, have a wide range of words covering the yellow to brown spectrum, and Eskimos can identify seventeen different variants of white[3]. The Maoris express a particular kind of perception in colour words for the different stages of plant growth, for forty different cloud formations, and use more than a hundred terms relating to red[4]. In Britain, as a part of our linguistic richness, we have inherited a remarkable number of words describing the colours of horses – roan, strawberry roan, bay, chestnut, grey, piebald, skewbald – as well as many terms applying to human hair colour: blond, brunette, grey, mousy, sandy, auburn, fair[5].

When colouring media were home-produced, slight variations in colour were inevitable and unimportant. The simple material names, such as 'Lead Colour' and 'Pearl Colour' used by a London paint merchant in the eighteenth century were adequately descriptive. But some of the names which succeeded them, responding more to fashion than to the product, could be totally misleading, thus the nineteenth century produced 'Rose Magdala' and 'Lyons Blue'. The 1950s dreamed up 'Blue Frost', 'Calypso' and 'Fire and Ice'; and the 1960s 'Tequila Sunrise', 'Kinky Pink', and 'Yellow Submarine'[6]. Manufacturers vie with one another to give interesting and memorable names for each new colour they produced, but this did not prevent 27 different American paint companies from producing their own different versions of 'Sky Blue', none of which matched that in the Textile Color Card of America[7]. Industrialisation of the textile, printing and paint industries highlighted the need for some form of effective colour description and communication.

Taking the primaries as a basis: red, yellow, and blue for pigment or red, green and blue for light, the early theorists arranged the colours in triangles, circles and polygons, linking the ends of the solar spectrum. Later, when it was realised that colour is determined by three dimensions: *hue* or colour (whether it is red, yellow or blue etc), *value* (lightness, brightness or reflectivity), and *chroma* (intensity or saturation), three-dimensional models were introduced. These included Lambert's colour pyramid (1772) and a cone and a sphere proposed by Wundt. The latter were the ancestors of the two popular systems of the twentieth century, the double cone of Ostwald and Munsell's sphere.

Both of these systems are expressed by a vertical axis representing the achromatic scale of lightness from black at the bottom to white at the top. (The terms lightness and brightness are roughly synomyous: lightness refers to light reflectance, brightness applies to colour as a property of a light source.) The axis is ringed at its central point of medium lightness by the hues arranged in spectral sequence at a corresponding lightness level. The radial steps back from the perimeter to the centre indicate the different degrees of saturation possible for each hue at the medium level of lightness. The pattern is repeated for each horizontal level of lightness; the closer to the circumference the more saturated the colour, the nearer to the centre the nearer to the neutral grey of the same lightness. The common feature of the figures: that of maximum girth at the centre tapering towards the poles, illustrates the fact that the greatest number of saturation steps between the pure hues and neutral grey occurs at the medium level of lightness; very dark and very light colours differ little from black and white[8]. The terms used to describe these three attributes of colour vary with the system. Munsell used the words *hue*, *value* and *chroma* with numbers to express the steps. Thus 5R 4/8 represents a red with a value of 4 (which is fairly dark) and a chroma of 8, a high degree of saturation. Geometric figures are inhibited by virtue of their fixed perimeters and Munsell developed his theoretical sphere into a 'tree' with irregular boundaries which accommodate

only those colours which are at present commercially obtainable. The 'branches' can be extended at each horizontal level to the full limits of colour discrimination.

A measurement system based upon optical matching was devised in 1880 by Joseph Lovibond, a Salisbury brewer, in response to complaints about his beer[9]. Supposedly inspired by the stained glass in the cathedral, Lovibond had the idea of colour-testing the beer against a series of brown glass filters. The invention proved successful, and he developed it into the Lovibond Tintometer, which can now be used visually to distinguish several million colour variations by different combinations of magenta, yellow and cyan, the three subtractive primary and additive secondary colours for light.

But the most practical systems for general purposes are those based upon the swatch principle: that is upon a series of colour chips or cards which can be reproduced in unlimited editions. The disadvantage is that of relying upon the techniques and colours of printing, usually on paper, to represent colours which may be applied on a very large scale to a wide variety of other materials. Applications to the various components of the building industry have been the concern of the British Building Research Establishment since the employment of the Munsell 'Archrome' range of 47 colours in the school building programme of the 1950s and 1960s. This has culminated in the British Standard (BS 5252) framework specifically developed for that purpose by a team working under the direction of H. L. Gloag[10]. Their principal objectives were: that all major 'hue regions' should be fully represented, that the identity of each hue should appear consistent and distinct from its neighbours at all levels of lightness and saturation, and that the hues chosen were to include as many mutual harmonies as possible. Although based upon the

1. *The relationship between this tile-hung cottage at Chiddingfold and its background is that of opposite or complementary colours; each stresses the intensity of the other.*

2. *The Munsell colour chart shows graded values from black to white, graded chromas of red, and a colour circle of ten hues at the strong degree of chroma or saturation which occurs at the equator of the colour sphere. (By permission of Munsell Color, Macbeth Division of Kollmorgan (UK) Ltd.)*

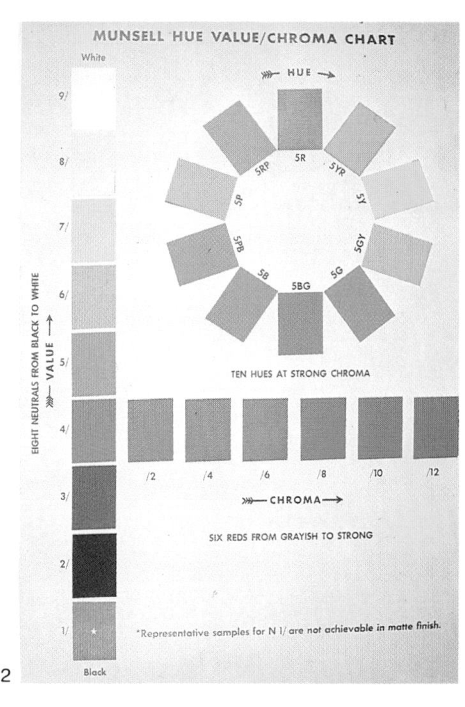

Munsell notation system, the classifications of *greyness* and *weight* were introduced to supplement the Munsell variables of chroma and value. The factor of greyness can more practically express the difference in apparent grey content between one colour and another and it enables colours to be organised into five categories arranged in vertical columns from grey to clear. The third factor, weight, refers to lightness or darkness and is a modification of value, the second factor in the Munsell system. In the British Standard BS 5252 framework the twelve hues are arranged horizontally, the greyness groups in five vertical columns, and the weight steps in varying numbers of subsidiary vertical columns within the greyness groups: a layout which is particularly useful in dealing with colour relationships. The framework overcomes certain limitations of the Munsell system in presenting a well-related range of colours for building purposes.

Confusingly, other countries have developed other systems. The US National Bureau of Standards, for instance, has adopted a naming method based on the Munsell system which divides the colour field up into about 300 main compartments, each described by a noun and up to three adjectives: for example 'dark greyish reddish brown' or 'moderate yellowish pink'[11]. By comparison the BS 5252 system is simplicity itself. Nevertheless, we cannot avoid the need to use words: for general descriptive purposes throughout this book, the dozen basic colour names will have to suffice.

1

2

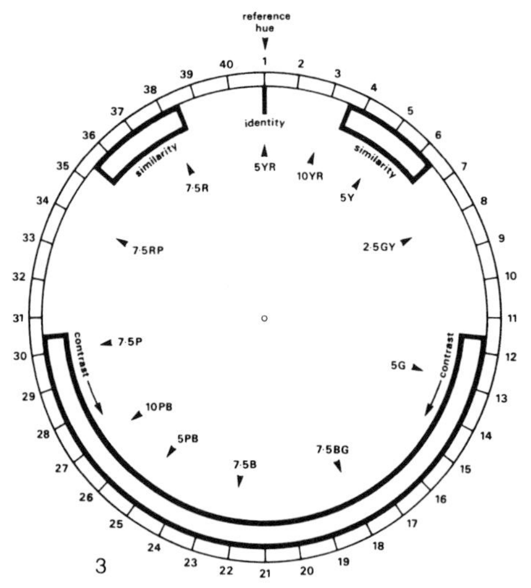

3

1. *The Munsell colour tree was developed from a colour sphere to accommodate the differences in value (lightness) and chroma (saturation) of which the various hues are capable. The number of branches is limited only by the practical difficulty of distinguishing between the variations in each of the three dimensions. (By permission of Munsell Color, Macbeth Division of Kollmorgan (UK) Ltd.)*

2. *Skeleton of Munsell colour tree showing the relationship of hue, value and chroma. (Drawn by Mark Lancaster.)*

3. *The harmonies of identity, similarity and contrast, separated by zones of ambiguity on a 40-step Munsell hue scale. This diagram (based on Moon and Spencer 1944) was developed by HL Gloag after detailed investigations of five leading theorists on the subject of harmony. The arrows show the relationship between one of the main framework hues and the other eleven in the BS 5252 Colour Co-ordination Framework. (Reproduced from the BRE Colour Coordination Handbook. Crown Copyright, by permission of the controller HMSO.)*

Colour harmony

Although it is generally supposed that certain colours may be combined in harmony or disharmony, and most theorists have set out to establish principles, the subject remains a controversial one. Fashion or usage undoubtedly plays an important role in colour selection and we may reflect upon the stages of the 'colour revolution' which has occurred in the western world during the nineteenth and twentieth centuries inducing us to absorb the colour palettes of many different cultures. Ostwald seems to have been expressing nineteenth-century attitudes when he condemned the large surfaces of pure vermilion found in Pompeii as crude and a discredit to the idea of the artistic superiority of the ancients[1]. Arnheim, although he produced his own theory, was cautious, suggesting that the principle on which many of the rules of colour harmony are based might be a recipe for dullness 'suitable at best for the so-called colour schemes of clothing or rooms'. Quoting Schoenberg, he observes that harmony is (with counterpoint and form) only one of the considerations in musical composition. 'If musical harmony were concerned only with the rules of what sounds well together, it would be limited to a kind of aesthetic etiquette. Instead of telling the musician by what means he can express what, it would teach him only how to behave.'[2] Hering noted that many great paintings do not have 'harmonious' combinations of colours[3]. Painters, with few exceptions, work mostly by intuition; and while we may gain valuable insights into the interpretation of the world and the effects of colour combinations, it is to the theorists that we must turn for ideas of harmony.

The first of these to produce a coherent set of principles was Chevreul, a chemist and director of the Gobelin tapestry works. In '*De la Loi du Contraste Simultane des Couleurs*', published in 1839[4], he identified six types of colour harmony: three of analogy and three of contrast. These may be summarised as: harmonies of adjacent, opposite, split-complementary and triadic colours, and that of a dominant tint.[5] Combinations of red, orange and yellow or blue, indigo and violet would represent harmonies of adjacent or analagous colours; those of red and green, yellow and purple, or blue and orange represent harmonies of opposite or complementary colours. The term split-complementaries refers to the colours immediately adjacent on either side of the opposite colour. Thus orange-red and yellow-orange are the split complementaries of blue, and yellow-orange and yellow-green, of purple. We must however remember that systems vary as well as nomenclature; Ostwald, for instance, places yellow – not orange – opposite to blue on his colour circle. Triadic colours are those in a triangular relationship at 120 degrees to one another on the colour circle. Examples are the primaries: red, yellow and blue, the secondaries: purple, orange and green, or the intermediates: red-orange, yellow-green, red-purple. Finally the harmony of a dominant tint is well portrayed in nature by the reflected light of the sky, by mist and fog, and above all by the enveloping yellow light of the sun.

Most theorists agree with Chevreul's general observation that colours look best together either when they are closely related (or analagous), complementary, or in strong contrast, and this has been confirmed by a number of studies in psychology[6]. Birren attributes to the first group an emotional quality arising out of their natural order, and to the second a visual quality. On the basis of investigations into the work of five different theorists Gloag concluded that harmony was primarily associated with hue rather than with the lightness or saturation of colours. It was moreover in the terms of Moon & Spencer's 'a clear-cut unambiguous relationship.'[7] Gloag and his team constructed an experimental 'hue-harmony selector' with a series of revolving discs which indicate three types of harmony: of *identity*, of *similarity*, and of *contrast*, separated by zones of *ambiguity* on a 40-step Munsell hue scale. From this a maximum of 5 harmonious hues can be obtained out of a total of 40 hue steps. The selector was intended not as an arbiter but as a guide in the selection of hues for the co-ordinating framework; but its readings have been found to conform reasonably well with the judgements of designers.[7]

Principles of harmony have also been applied to colours produced by relating single hues to black, white and grey. These were described in a triangle produced by Ewald Hering, a German physiologist, around 1878. With a single hue at one corner and black and white at the others, it is possible to plot all transitions of the hue in *shades* towards black along one side, in *tints* towards white along the other, and in *tones* towards grey across the middle in each direction; grey being already at the mid-point of the third side between black and white. It is a beautifully simple method of linking each hue with the achromatic absolutes in large numbers of sequential steps. Birren has developed this into a series of colour figures, offering a wide range of possibilities. He also draws attention to

1

2

3

4

5

what he calls 'the New Perception' concerned with modes of appearance, such as lustre, iridescence, luminosity and transparency, all of which feature increasingly in late twentieth century uses of colour[8].

Judgements of harmony between small, 'captive' areas of colour in a similar format are however very different from those in the field where we are concerned with great differences in size, with much more subtle and complex combinations of colours, and with the effects of constantly changing light. The addition of scale to any principles of harmony would make them so complex as to be unworkable. But it is a vital factor, acknowledged by both Ostwald and Munsell who have suggested that highly saturated colours should be confined to small surfaces, and large surfaces should have subdued colours[9]. As a general guiding principle this may be valid, but the matter cannot be decided without reference to all the other factors, including the subject, the context, and human perception.

Harmonies of analogy

1. *The close relationship between the red of the roofs, the pinkish colour of the walls and the reddish yellow of the grass, in these houses at Swindon, is immediately appealing. The effect is spoilt by the highly reflective white gable.*

2. *The red roofs and the red and pink walls of these houses at Petworth relate closely to the yellowish-brown of the ploughed field.*

Harmonies of contrast

3. *The red roofs and green fields are complementary, but the contrast is softened by the intervening beige of the walls. Dunbar, Scotland.*

4. *The contrast between the reddish-yellow house wall and the green grass is less extreme than if it were red. The house is also weighed down by the dark slate roof, a good landscape colour. Petworth, Sussex.*

Ambiguity

5. *Natural greens are much more complex than the crude greens that we are able to provide in painted buildings, which often have an ambiguous relationship with their landscape surroundings. The reflective capacity of the roof is notable in this view. Ditchling, Sussex. (Photograph by Tom Turner)*

Colour perception and association

When we look at a tree in the cold light of dawn or against the setting sun, it may appear grey or black, but we know that it is green. Similarly, we know that a white object by candlelight is white although it appears yellow. This phenomenon, known as *colour constancy* (illustrated by the different views of the Thames on pages 10 & 11), is one of the difficulties in understanding colour[1]. Pure colour, in fact, can normally be seen only in the controlled conditions of the laboratory, where it appears 'filmy and insubstantial at an indefinite distance'[2]. In the world outside colours appear to be localised as part of the surfaces on which they are seen: their perception reveals a 'regression towards the real object'[3].

The red colour of blood, brick, hair or a flower, may be under certain circumstances *visually* indistinguishable, but *perceptibly* they seem quite different. Specialists such as painters are aware of this, albeit sometimes dimly, because of their need to reproduce the actual colours seen; even so they can never see the colours divorced from their surrounding or background colours. In general we tend to think of self-coloured materials in terms of their substance rather than their colour, and regard only applied colours, the specific eyecatching colours of paints and plastics, as colours.

The different ways in which we appreciate colours has been the subject of considerable study. Children generally have been found to prefer bright colours, but the preferences of adults are much less tractable. Itten, on assigning 'harmonic' colour combinations to a class of young art students in 1928, was surprised to discover that they found his harmonies discordant. They proceeded to find their own, which displayed considerable differences from one another, particularly in terms of saturation or intensity (chroma). This phenomenon he called *subjective timbre*, which expresses in some degree the nature of the person[4].

As research into the functioning of the brain advances it is beginning to reveal a high degree of complexity in the response to colour. It is now known that the cerebral hemispheres are responsible for contrasting attitudes to information. The left side is 'the centre of verbal and mathematical ability, the seat of logic and rational deduction', while the right side (which incidentally has a coarser cell and nerve struc-

1, 2. *The ephemeral nature of colour is revealed in these two views of the Renault Centre at Swindon, taken from opposite directions with and against the sun.*

1

2

1

2

3

4

5

6

ture) is efficient at processing abstract, non-verbal information. It responds to texture and colour, and deals with spatial perception and patterns of coherence. 'Though the visceral brain (limbic system) could never aspire to conceive of the colour red in terms of a three-letter word or a specific wavelength of light, it could associate the colour symbolically with such diverse things as blood, fainting, fighting, flowers, etc.'[5].

It is beginning to look as though the brain responds to colour basically in three different ways. The right hemisphere seems to be concerned only with those colours outside the limited range of the primary and exotic, being responsive to the more subtle 'cerebral' or 'sophisticated' colours. The limbic system, on the other hand, (which is responsible for the exteriorisation of emotion), responds in two ways: to high chroma, brightness and glitter; secondly it is concerned with symbolic associations with archteypal origins. Smith suggests that it is a characteristic of great art to generate a critical tension between these cerebral and emotional responses, and a failure of contemporary architecture that it relies too heavily upon the cerebral, equating the emotional with vulgarity. 'For limbic satisfaction it is necessary to go to market places, Piccadilly Circus or Las Vegas.'[6] While we would not all choose Las Vegas – or even Piccadilly Circus – as environmental models, the statement rings true.

1, 2, 3. *Colour assimilation. Seen from a distance the colours of the individual bricks and of their mortar joints become assimilated into a single overall colour. In this case the brick colours are similar, but the mortar colours are different, giving different overall assimilated colour effects.*

4, 5, 6. *The blue house has many interesting faces, according to the light. Dull weather stresses its coolness* **4**. *The low sunlight warms the blue, or turns it orange* **5, 6**. *The two pictures were taken simultaneously early on an August evening.*

Colour effects

One of the difficulties of understanding the properties of colour is the fact that pure colour can only be seen in the form of light. The colours which we customarily call primaries, because they cannot be reproduced by mixing other colours, are based upon pigment compounds which absorb red, yellow and blue light rays. In fact pigments are impure and in any case, as Moses Harris pointed out as long ago as 1766[1] the mixture of these three will produce only a very limited range of colours: The artist requires many more pigments such as vermilion, cadmium orange, lemon yellow, ultramarine and cobalt, as well as colours produced by other processes. In considering colour and its effects we are thus considering light; in illustrating those effects we are considering pigments.

Beams of red, green and blue light mix to produced white light. These are known as the *additive* or light primaries. Two of them mixed together will produce the *additive secondaries:* magenta (a bluish red), yellow and cyan (a greenish blue). These are also known as the *subtractive primaries* because, where they overlap the three additive primaries: red, green and blue appear as *subtractive secondaries*. Where a disc is placed to throw a shadow in one of the mingled beams of red, green and blue light, it subtracts a primary colour from the mixture. Where it subtracts red the shadow will be cyan, where it subtracts green the shadow will be magenta, and where it subtracts blue the shadow will be yellow. Where all three are subtracted the shadow will be black[2].

Red has the longest wavelength and the lowest energy of all visible light, it is the 'hottest' of the warm colours and nearest to the wavelength of infra-red. Red is the first colour to be perceived by babies and invariably the first to be described in the development of language. It has the greatest emotional impact of all the colours, quickening the heart-rate and causing adrenalin to flow[3]. It has universal associations with blood, war, revolution, danger, anger and love and is frequently used in connection with religion, royalty and aristocratic pursuits. Unlike blue and yellow which appear to 'spread', red seems to contract: a fact which is thought by some investigators to be due to the way in which the cone pigments are distributed on the retina[4]. Red also has the characteristic of appearing to advance, in contrast to blue, which seems to retreat. This may be because the natural focal point of red light waves falls behind the retina; that of blue waves in front.[5]

Blue, in contrast to red, is calming, or at the extreme, depressing. Like most colours, it has an ambivalence of association. Apart from its elusive presence in the sky and sea the colour is relatively rare in nature, which is perhaps why blue buildings often look uncomfortable in the landscape. Although blue flowers are common their colour is often inclined towards red or purple. It occurs in blue eyes, the feathers of a few birds, and some insects, in fish but in very few animals. Underground it is rarer: the only mineral blues are lapis lazuli, turquoise and azurite, a compound of copper which is likely to turn green when extracted. Both copper and cobalt need technology to extract the blues, and the natural vegetable dyes, indigo and woad, used to be called hidden colours on account of the need for a chemical reaction to reveal any colour at all. Ultramarine, literally 'from over the sea', was processed from lapis lazuli. In the Middle Ages, when it was used for illuminating manuscripts, it was as precious as gold. Since then it has been chemically synthesised as 'washing blue'[6].

Yellow is the most reflective of the true colours (after the achromatic white) and it is the most easily seen. Like red it appears to advance. It is unique among the hues in that it is brightest when fully saturated, whereas the others become darker; when yellow darkens it ceases to appear yellow. Pure spectral yellow occupies only a narrow band of the spectrum compared with the other primary colours. Most of the yellow light comes from a mixture of red and green light. Yellow occurs commonly in nature: in minerals such as sulphur, as gold, and as orpiment, a sulphide of arsenic, which was an important pigment in the ancient world. It is also a colour, with reds and browns, produced by iron in the earth, a strong component of surface geology. Yellow pigments can be produced from ochres, yellow marls and sands, all of which contain limonite[7]. The colour occurs most strikingly in London Stock bricks. It occurs dramatically in many insects, reptiles, birds and fish and less so, but commonly, in animals. Yellow permeates the vegetable world, being one of the commonest flower colours, and it occurs as a component of the greens of spring and beiges and browns of summer and autumn. In its benign aspect is is an expression of joy and sunlight; but there is also a dark side associated with greed, cowardice and betrayal – Judas Iscariot was often portrayed in yellow robes.

Green has a reputation for being the most restful colour, and it is the most easily seen. Its

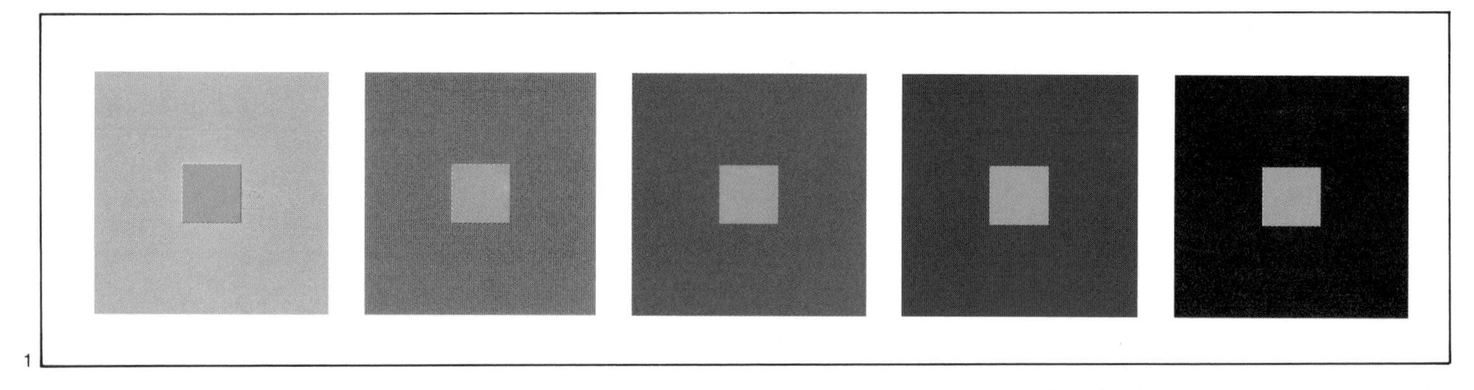

1

2 3

4

5

wavelengths focus almost exactly upon the retina. When the majority of the colour receptor cells are working together in daylight they are thought to be most sensitive to yellowish-green light[8]. Green is however a difficult colour to reproduce. Although there are a number of green rocks, including serpentine and slate, there are few green minerals. Until about fifty years ago chemical synthesis produced only murky and pale greens with poor light fastness[9]. Rare in the earth, green is supreme as the colour of vegetation, essential in the form of the pigment chlorophyll for photosynthesis. It is a common colour among

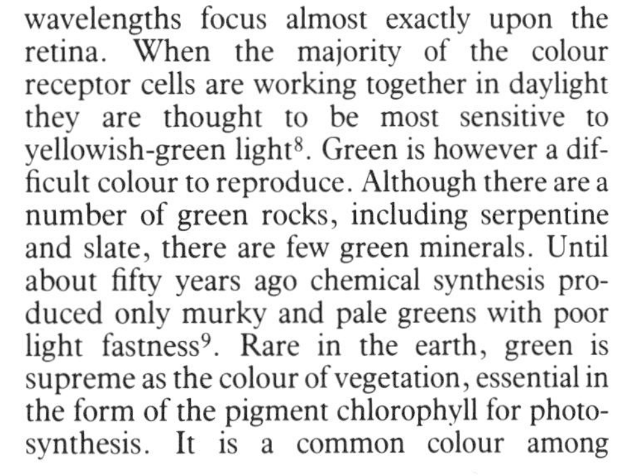

1. *The eye concentrating on the colour of one of the outer squares will simultaneously generate its complementary colour in the central grey square. That on the yellow square will appear purple, that on orange will appear blue and that on red will appear green. The converse effect will occur on the opposite squares. (Illustration by Barbara Lang after Johannes Itten.)*

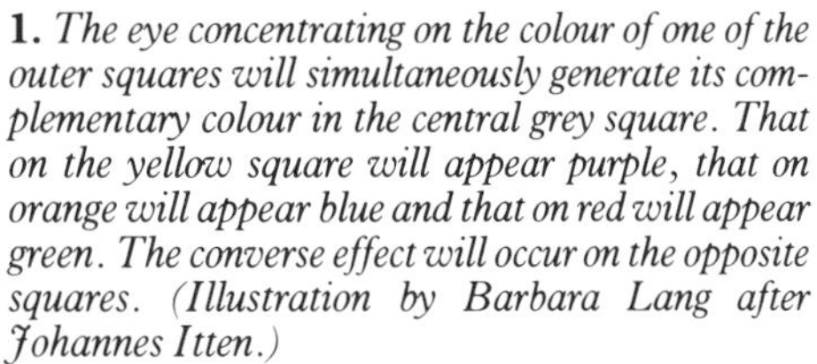

2, 3. *Colours appear different according to those adjoining: an effect which is exploited in the use of 'advancing' red and 'receding' blue tiles, each related to yellow on this Edwardian garden path. The colour is reduced by reflected light when viewed from an angle. (Photographs by Stephen Lancaster.)*

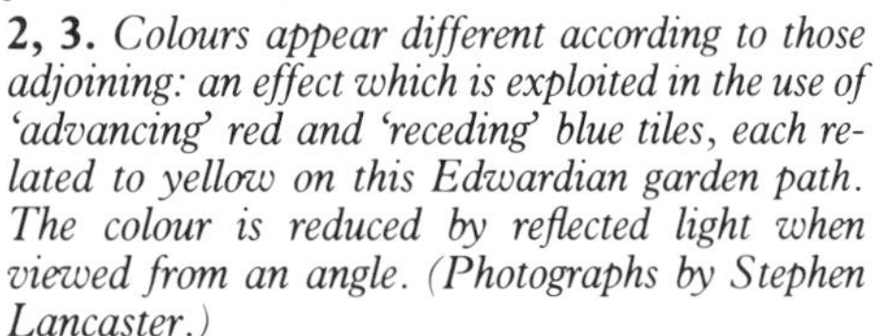

4. *The rainwater has intensified the colours of the red and blue paving bricks except where it acts as a mirror reflecting the light. Kew Palace, London.*

5. *The wet road becomes a mirror in which the sky is white and the white gate appears black. Wales.*

6. *Sometimes even near objects are transformed by light. Light and colour become so dominant that the object itself is reduced to insignificance. Perception of this transformation has been described as a change from the object mode to the illuminant mode of colour appearance. Newcastle.*

reptiles, some birds, and many insects.

No colour, in the world outside the laboratory, is ever seen in isolation, but always in relation to others, whether they be specifically applied colours or the incidental colours of materials. This relationship of a colour to its background is called *colour attachment*. Thus the colour of a signboard or a building, or even a door, will have an attachment to its background colour. While opinions differ on the specific colour relationship; whether it be analagous or contrasting, ambiguity should be avoided. Some degree of contrast is an important – indeed vital – attribute of colour, which sustains our interest and helps us find our way in the world. *Ambiguity* taken to its limits would give us a nightmare world in which everything was camouflaged. In fact relatively few creatures and plants have this attribute, and traditional buildings are more often distinguished by their contrasts. 'Harmony is a clear-cut, unambiguous relationship.'[10]

Itten recognises seven categories of colour contrast[11]: hue, light-dark, cold-warm, complementary, simultaneous, saturation and extension. The strongest *contrast of hues* occurs with the primary hues: red, yellow and blue; it diminishes as the hues move away from the primaries. *Light-dark contrast* is well illustrated by the contrast between day and night, white and black, or, more subtly, the two primary hues yellow and blue. Similarly blue and yellow, or more strongly blue and red, express a *cold-warm contrast*. The *contrast of complementary pairs:* red-green, yellow-purple, blue-orange, represents the extreme of opposition. As Itten says: 'they incite each other to maximum vividness when adjacent; and they annihilate each other, to grey-black, when mixed.'

Simultaneous contrast,[12] may be seen in the differing appearance of the same colour on different backgrounds: a grey object for example, looks darker against a light background than it does against a darker background; also it explains the apparently dark edges of successive ranges of hills seen against the light. It is the spontaneous generation of the complementary for any given colour, if it is not present; it describes a chromatic shift towards the complementary of any two colours that are not precisely complementary. *Saturation contrast* is 'the contrast between pure, intense colours and dull, diluted colours.' *Contrast of extension* is the contrast of area. Since the primary colours all have distinctly different characteristics – yellow is the lightest with the highest reflectivity, red has the highest intensity and blue is the most recessive – some kind of balance needs to be established. Goethe proposed simple numerical ratios: yellow: 9, orange: 8, red: 6, violet: 3, blue: 4 and green: 6, giving ratios for complementary pairs: yellow:violet at 3:1, orange:blue 2:1, and red:green at 1:1[13].

6

The question of balance is explored in the paintings of Mondrian, and to some extent in the architecture of Rietveldt. It is of fundamental importance in the use of environmental colour, and it is necessary to draw clear distinctions between the use of large coloured surfaces, or deliniation of outline or detail with strong colour. These are distinguished by J. P. Lenclos in a number of detailed colour analyses carried out in various part of the world, as *palette générale* and *palette punctuale*[14]. It may be noted that in the natural world the strongest colours are usually confined to small areas; large areas of highly saturated colour are rare.

As the eye adapts by dilation in moving from a light area to a dark one, to admit more light, it adapts from one colour to another. Two colours juxtaposed will cause the eye to move from one when it has become saturated, and then back again. Such effects can be used to create a sensation of flicker or movement[15], which has been exploited by the exponents of Op Art, and before them the designers of Victorian and Edwardian tile patterns. Advancing and recessive colours can be used, and the colours can be employed in different patterns and on different surfaces. Britain has so far consciously produced few recent environmental examples comparable to those in Europe and the USA[16]. The advertising industry has however created some exciting short-lived effects by used modulations of lightness and intensity of different hues achieved by a computor printing process, in some cigarette advertising posters[17]. In these the pictures present themselves at a distance as though through a heat haze; as one approaches the blur increases and the image gives way to an abstract series of coloured squares. At a distance the colours begin to merge to produce the required images. At greater distances the images themselves would merge into uniform areas of colour. In a similar way, by the process known as *colour assimilation*, the colour of the mortar of a brick wall seen at a distance, will merge with the colour of the bricks, coalescing into a uniform colour[18].

All things seen from a distance, as for instance from a high-flying aeroplane, are first seen not as objects, but as disembodied patches of colour. But in the real world these are rarely isolated; they jostle for attention, sometimes so much that we are overwhelmed by the sheer complexity of the scene and long 'to get away from it all'. The complexity increases with the scale, and the simplest colour relationships are liable to become confused by the wide variety of materials employed in the most subtle and complex of backgrounds, that of the natural world.

The geography of colour

A view of the different regions of the earth reveal a predominance of one or more basic colours. White, for instance, relieved by the greys and greens of water, characterises the landscape of the polar regions; green the temperate regions, and brown the desert regions. Buildings like the igloo may have complete affinity with their background, blending as it does both in colour and in form. More commonly, as in many indiginous buildings in different parts of the world, the colour will have an affinity but the form will be distinct. Mud, the basic building material in most parts of the world, in common with such materials as wood and thatch, expresses both in its organic flexibility and its natural colour a fundamental relationship with the land. But mud buildings need protection from the weather, particularly around their edges and openings, and these are frequently the first areas to be painted, the paint perhaps being white, or coloured, drawing attention to the special significance of doors, windows and parapets. Sometimes the linear technique would extend as a pattern over the surface, particularly of important buildings; sometimes it would cover the whole surface, sometimes both. As mud buildings were once common, either in the form of mud brick, mud-rendered rubble, or wattle and daub combined with timber framing, it is likely that some form of colourwash or distemper was also much more widespread. The tradition has survived and developed with the use of cement renders.

Stone also has a special relationship with the landscape. Because transport costs were always prohibitive, except for important buildings of religious and social significance, indiginous stone buildings act as indicators of their geological parentage, occasionally revealed in matching outcrops. This is particularly apparent in Britain where one can scarcely travel thirty miles without crossing a geological boundary. Thus it is possible to define many areas of specific and coherent character by their buildings and landscape background. Our 12 national parks and 24 Areas of Outstanding Natural Beauty give focus to this character, but it has many subtle expressions in the areas in between. While the buildings of Dartmoor and the Cotswolds are simply expressed in stone, areas of geological transition have fascinating combinations of stone, brick and timber. Brick, which is seldom the colour of the earth from which it is moulded, nevertheless has local affinities, and the brick colours of vernacular buildings are often associated with specific localities. This practice could be extended much more to new buildings, in which, for a variety of reasons, both local precedent and the subtle potential of brickwork are often ignored. Flexibility of use and variety of colour are the essence of fine brickwork. Although most bricks are now machine-made, there is a wide variety of colours to choose from, including many still available in hand-made bricks.

Planning authorities give advice and place restraints upon the uses of colour, particularly in connection with National Parks and Conservation Areas. But there is a need for coherent policies based on the identification of the essential colour character of all areas. Such an identification has been undertaken in France by Jean-Philippe Lenclos, an international colour consultant. Lenclos has established a methodology based upon the natural and man-made elements of the area. From samples of earth, rock, plants, building materials and flakes of paint, from related drawings, he carefully builds up 'chromatic palettes'. These are then translated into a series of *palettes régionales* which provide the foundation for future proposals.

The character of the landscape itself is expressed in the land form and the pattern and colour of its incident. In the natural landscape this is the pattern of erosion and vegetation. In the almost ubiquitous man-made landscape of Britain today it is the pattern of forest and woodland, field and hedgerow, and farm buildings, villages and towns, all of which express colour. This occurs as mineral colour in ploughland and areas of exposed rock, and to a large extent in buildings. It is the predominant colour of the town. Vegetable colour is the principal colour of the countryside, but it also plays an important role in the town, occasionally giving the town its own special image. We associate the plane tree with London and Paris and the lime with Berlin. In Africa and India some towns are momentarily transformed by the flowering of the flame trees, the blue jacaranda, and the yellow cassia. But the most dramatic way in which colour occurs, is when it is applied in the form of paint or other coloured materials. In this deliberate and often creative application we are the inheritors of many traditions, in which function, symbolism and decoration are inextricably mixed. Symbolism undoubtedly played a vital part in past civilisations, as it still does in some cultures; to what extent it inspires surviving colour traditions and how much they are simply the result of our impulse to create, we can only guess.

1

2

3

1. *Kano, Nigeria. In 1960, when this picture was taken from the minaret of the mosque, no tower blocks had been built in this southern Saharan city. All the buildings are of sun-dried bricks plastered over with mud dug on site, leaving 'borrow-pits' which form small ponds during the rainy season. Most houses are plain but some have whitewashed door and window surrounds, some more important ones have façades decorated in relief and 'dog-ear' finials at the corners. The round buildings are reception rooms, transition zones between the private family quarters and the world outside.*

2. *Stone has a special relationship with the landscape. The brown stone with which these village houses in the Cantabrian mountains of Northern Spain are built suggests an immediate relationship with the craggy mountains beyond.*

3. *Although it looks like a red brick and tile town in this view from the abbey tower, the old trading town of Tewkesbury, sited at the confluence of the rivers Severn and Avon, is still noted for its half-timbered buildings.*

Symbolic and creative colour

In pre-literate societies colours were important in that they gave a sense of orientation, both literal and psychological. Various societies have used them to indicate directions, a practice which survives among the Pueblo and Cherokee indians of North America. To one Pueblo tribe, north is yellow, south red, east white, west blue, and up and down are symbolised by either black or variegated colours. But the colours are not universal: they vary from tribe to tribe. To the Cherokee both directions and colours have direct associations with the human condition. Blue means north and trouble, white means south and happiness, red is the colour of the east and success, and black is that of the west and death[1]. Perhaps the directions are linked in folk memory with actual experiences; we still believe that black is an appropriate colour for death. In Imperial Rome, however, in parts of India, and in nationalist China, white – not black – has been used to represent mourning. We refer to our aristocracy as being 'blue-blooded'; to the Maya Indians, the blood of kings was white[2].

The four elements – fire, air, water and earth – were represented in the Old Testament by red, blue, purple and white respectively; flames combining these colours symbolised the presence of God[3]. In ancient Egypt the heavens were blue and the fertile banks of the Nile were green; these colours were used with others to decorate religious and secular objects according to a prescribed hierarchy. Dreams were also symbolised by colour. Their significance was measured by the prominence of a particular colour: red for example, signified ardent love, but when mixed with black it signified hatred[4].

The preoccupation with astronomy and astrology inevitably identified colours with the planets and this was expressed in the ziggurats. The archaeologist Leonard Woolley describes the 4500 year old 'Mountain God' at Ur in Mesopotania as built in stages, the lowest wall being black to represent the underworld and the upper wall red to represent the habitable earth. At the top a blue-tiled shrine was roofed in gold, symbolising the sun. Another example is the fourth century BC city of Ectabana described by Herodotus as a construction in layers from white at the base, through black, red, blue and orange, to gold and silver at its peak. Similarly there are indications that the buildings of the Inca, Maya and Toltec cultures of South America were brightly coloured[5]. In the ancient Chinese capital city of Peking, it seems that colour was used to express both the supernatural and the social orders. The walls were red, symbolising benign forces, and the roofs generally made of blue glazed tiles. But the Imperial Palace was roofed in yellow tiles of a shade associated with malign influences, in order to 'camouflage' the buildings against any evil spirits passing overhead. The bricks and tiles of ordinary buildings outside were specially fired to a drab colour so as not to compete[6]. From such records and hypotheses we learn much about symbolism and the social order, but little about the use of colour for architectural expression. For this we need to look to Greece.

The Minoan civilisations of Crete on the one hand made use of colour in murals and, on the other, a sophisticated use of simple bold colours on their lintels, capitals and columns; seen in Sir Arthur Evans's reconstruction of Knossos in 1926. Although less strident in their use of strong colours than is sometimes supposed, the Hellenic Greeks appear to have developed the use of colour in much the same way as they corrected the optical distortions in stone. This is apparent in the use of two or more different graduated blues to accentuate the shapes of some Ionian capitals, as well as those of the triglyphs on the Parthenon, suggesting shadows. The Parthenon frieze itself, brightly coloured in blues, red, gold and flesh-colour, as re-constructed in the Ontario Museum[7], seems to combine something of the functions of narrative art with those of advertising in its dramatic recording of heroic events. We might also regard some of the more colourful manifestations of Christianity, which occurred some nineteen centuries later, in this way.

The Romans were more concerned with building materials and techniques than with painting buildings externally. But the imperial building programme created an unprecedented demand for decoration. This was expressed in two ways: mural painting for the walls and mosaics for the floors. The first developed into the tradition of narrative painting which has spread all over Europe, and has recently been revived in our 'street art'. The art of mosaics moved up from the floor to flourish on the walls and domes of the early Christian churches of the Byzantine Empire, and later, combined with the ceramic tile, found expression in the highly formalised decorations of Islamic mosques.

The faint traces of murals that remain give little hint of the colour that was once associated with the Christian church. For that we need to refer to the interiors of some French churches,

1

2

3

Traditional palettes

1, 2, 3. *Mexico has developed colour traditions from both the Indian and the Spanish cultures, including ceramic tile-work and colour-wash. The latter is seen at its most vibrant in the former garrison town of Guanajuato, capital of the central state of that name. The old centre of this large metropolis has recently been upgraded into Mexico's first conservation area which is now controlled by the supervisor of Ancient Monuments. There is a strong preference for reds and yellows, with mouldings and openings picked out in white, and plinths sometimes very practically coloured deep red or brown. The temporary bleaching effect of the strong sun can be clearly seen in the contrast between the intensity of shaded colours compared with those in direct sunlight. (Photographs by Heather Blackett)*

to some of our own highly coloured tomb monuments, and, perhaps most of all, to the bright portrayals of the Christian narrative in some of the ikons and murals of the eastern orthodox church. Investigations have revealed extensive traces of colour on the outsides of several French cathedrals, including red stain on the stone of Nôtre Dame in Paris, and red, blue and green at Angers, suggesting effects akin to some of the surviving interiors. But England also used colour, as recent stone restorations at Wells have revealed. Cecil Stewart describes these in *Gothic Architecture*[8]. Wells had: 'one hundred and seventy-six full-length statues . . . brilliantly coloured. The niches were dark red, and the figures and drapery were painted in yellow ochre, with eyes and hair picked out in black and the lips in red. In the central group of the Virgin and Child, the Virgin's robe was black with a green lining, while the Child's robe was crimson, the composition being set on a background of red and green diaper. there is evidence from plugholes, that the statues were further enriched with gilded metal ornament. Above, the rows of angels were painted rosy red.'

Such applied colour could not last in the English climate, nor in the climate of austerity which came with the Reformation, and later with Puritanism. The architects of the Renaissance largely dispensed with colour, relying upon dramatic shadows produced by strong form and texture. But this initially had little effect upon the traditions of folk art and vernacular building, both of which have colourful traditions.

Venice, where traditionally the orient began, has long been associated with colour, and the customs of hanging coloured rugs out of the windows of St Mark's Square at festival times has persisted. Even without this adornment the façades are colourful and are often treated like paintings, being decorated with different coloured patterns of marble[9]. On the island of Burano, across the lagoon, a different tradition endures. The houses, and even parts of houses occupied by particular families, are painted in a wide range of strong colours: pink, purple, red, orange, green, blue, brown, grey and black, all unified by white window and door surrounds and green shutters. When it is time for repainting the family concerned usually chooses a colour similar to that existing, although often brighter, to paint only the part of the block which it occupies. In this way, with the encouragement of the local authority, scale is main-

1

tained, as well as individuality; also, most important, the workings of time are in evidence[10]. Similar traditions associated with small close-knit fishing communities, where there is a tradition of painting boats, are found in many parts of the world. They can be seen on the Mediterranean island of Procida and on a number of Greek islands, as well as the surrounding mainlands. But they are not always colour traditions. On the island of Ibiza, for example, the buildings are mostly white, colour typically being limited to the door and window surrounds of some farm houses. The 'white' tradition, shared by many towns and villages of Moorish influence, is not however, strong on the adjacent island of Majorca where better building stone was available. Traditions of white or colour wash are most common where there is a reliance on mud, plaster, or render to weatherproof the walls. But we should not discount the other influences. One is undoubtedly the classical tradition which favoured the use of dressed stone, or its substitute, stucco; another is simply the impulse to colour, which we can see in many vernacular examples, from the red-painted clapboard barns of Iowa to the brightly stained fisherman's houses of Scandinavia. The painted plaster traditions in Central and South America have both folk and classical origins and exhibit several different 'palettes'. Few are as dramatic as the town of Guanajuato, Mexico's first conservation area.

Original colours are the subject of much controversy and very little research. We know that Turin yellow originated – or at least was promoted – in 1800, and that the Empress Maria Theresa gave her name to the use of a yellow in Vienna, now seen in the Heiligenkreuzerhof[11]; but there are few records which give any useful information on more rural traditions. Today's colours are predominantly warm; the commonest colours in most parts of the world being reds and yellows and their derivatives. Lenclos in his colour study of France illustrates relatively few examples of cool colours[12]. Notable exceptions are the 'blue' villages of North Africa, the predominance of blue window surrounds in some parts of Spain, and some blue villages in the Carpathian mountains of Poland. In the former cases the colour is appropriate to the climate; in the last it is said to be used as an insect repellant.

The reasons for rendering and for whitewashing are clear; those for colour washing much less so. Undoubtedly, colours changed according to, say, the need for redecoration, personal wealth, custom, and availability of pigments. They must also have faded with the weather; in Britain much more than in the countries of the south. Nevertheless even in Britain, there are strong traditions surviving, particularly in areas poor in building materials such as Suffolk, but also in other areas. Until the seventeenth century, when most houses in England were built of wood, largely with wattle and daub infilling, the tradition must have been much more widespread.

1–5. *Burano, Italy. As in many fishing ports, the tradition of painting boats has spread to the houses, expressing in Burano an amazing degree of individuality in choice of colours. Almost every hue seems to be represented and drawn together to a remarkable degree by the white of door and window surrounds and green of shutters. When it is time for repainting, the family concerned usually chooses a hue similar to that existing, although often brighter, to paint only the part of the block which it occupies. In this way, with the encouragement of the local authority, the scale as well as individuality is maintained and most important, the workings of time are in evidence. (Photographs by Biagio Guccione)*

6, 7. *Procida. The ravages of time are only too apparent on the island of Procida, off the coast of Naples, the harbour of which is dominated by tall vaulted houses with a distinctly arab flavour. Here pink, white and cream are the preferred colours, with some orange and yellow. The highly reflective colours can be seen for a long way out to sea.*

2

3

4

5

6

7

1

2

3

4

5

6

7

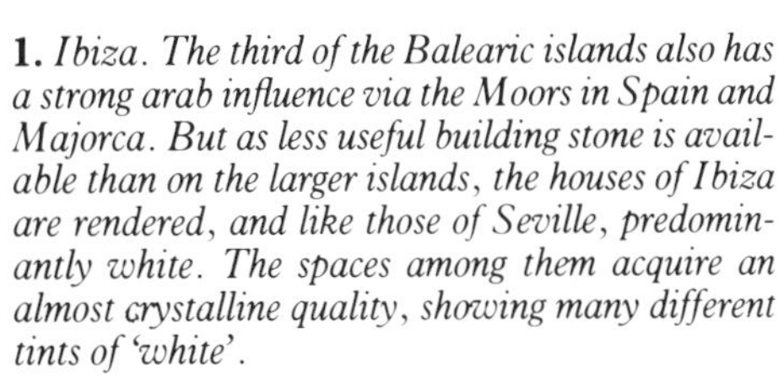

1. *Ibiza. The third of the Balearic islands also has a strong arab influence via the Moors in Spain and Majorca. But as less useful building stone is available than on the larger islands, the houses of Ibiza are rendered, and like those of Seville, predominantly white. The spaces among them acquire an almost crystalline quality, showing many different tints of 'white'.*

2. *Where most of the buildings are white, an unusual red building acquires a special significance, Ibiza.*

3. *Highly saturated red and yellow ochres mark the houses in the square of this eastern Spanish town.*

4–7. *Austria. The chalky pastel colours of the Baroque, strongly framed by white, give a cool refined atmosphere to some of the small towns overlooking the river Inn above Passau.*

Traditional building in Britain

A painter, trained to look at colour, is likely to see first the 'redness' of a brick building, but for most of us it is the sense of the material that is immediately apparent. By a peculiarity of perception we cannot easily divorce colours from materials to which they are seen to belong[1]. While most of us are aware of a great richness of building materials covering a wide range of colours, we do not tend to think of British building traditions particularly in terms of colour. The one exception is that of colour wash, the freshly coloured cottages scattered about the country and concentrated in the small towns and villages of East Anglia, Somerset and Devon; these relics of a time when the majority of houses throughout the country were built of wood and mud. London, until the great fire was a half-timbered city; Manchester remained so until well into the eighteenth century, and in some areas timber houses were still being built at the beginning of the nineteenth century[2].

Britain is basically a land of forest, and timber was for a long time the commonest building material. Even now we depend upon it for most of our roofs, floors, doors and many of our windows. Now it is mostly imported, but it was once so common that people in the Weald could refer to the oak as 'the Sussex weed'. Most building timber was cultivated in the woodlands which covered a large part of the country. In the thirteenth century there were in addition 60 officially recorded forests, totalling well over 4 million acres. By the seventeenth century, the demands of ship-building and iron smelting, as well as indiscriminate felling, had reduced the acreage to about 3 million; of which remnants survive at Sherwood, Epping, Dean and Cannock, and in the name of Enfield Chase[3].

Oak was the best building timber, being strong, close-grained and very durable. It is however difficult to fell and harder to work than most other timbers, and ordinary houses were often built of softer woods such as chestnut, elm, hornbeam and willow. This, coupled with the fact that the increasing wealth of the country from the sixteenth century onward enabled more people to build in oak, has led to the impression that all timber buildings were of this wood[4]. Its remarkable durability allowed it either to be plastered over or left exposed to weather. But it is likely that the frame and panels were in many cases painted over as one surface. Alternatively the frame would be expressed, accompanied by a high degree of decoration in the bridging members, carved jetties and other details. The practice of painting them black to contrast with the white infill panels – giving rise to the descriptive name 'magpie-houses' – derives from the nineteenth century, when tar became commercially available. This has now become the common practice in the west of England; in the east they are more often creosoted brown, or left to weather to a gentle grey. By contrast, the timber frames of central and northern Europe, including some of softer woods such as fir and pine, were painted, and they add a strong element of colour to the half-timbered towns of France and Germany.[5]. These can be seen sometimes elaborately carved and painted in a variety of colours, with a predominance of reds, browns and black.

Basically, two methods of timber construction were used in Britain: the 'cruck' and the 'box-frame'. The cruck is an A-frame which transfers the roof load directly to the ground. The roof load on the box-frame is transferred via the frame and walls to the ground. Cruck construction was normal in northern England, the Midlands and Wales. It was often chosen for the more important buildings such as tithe-barns. Box-frame construction was common in all parts of the country, with local variations in the quantity and sizes of the timbers used. This is most evident in the difference in spacing between the vertical timbers. The commonest form is that in which the main frames are set wide apart with roughly square or rectangular panels between them with subsidiary concealed studding used as a base for the infilling material.

The most elegant are those built between the late fifteenth and the beginning of the seventeenth century; with the studs closely spaced and long narrow panels between them, clearly designed to be looked at. In places it was carried to extremes of elaboration both in pattern and carved detail. Pevsner comments that the well-to-do clothiers of Shrewsbury at the end of the sixteenth century still preferred timber to stone 'because it made possible a more ostentatious display and allowed certain fineries of which in stone they would not have been capable.'[6].

Mud, the other material in common use, was employed in a variety of ways. At the basic level, mud lumps or unfired clay bricks were used to build thick 'cob' walls of the kind still found in Devon. Wattle-and-daub was the material most commonly used for infilling the panels between the timber frames. This comprised a mixture of clay, dung, or horsehair

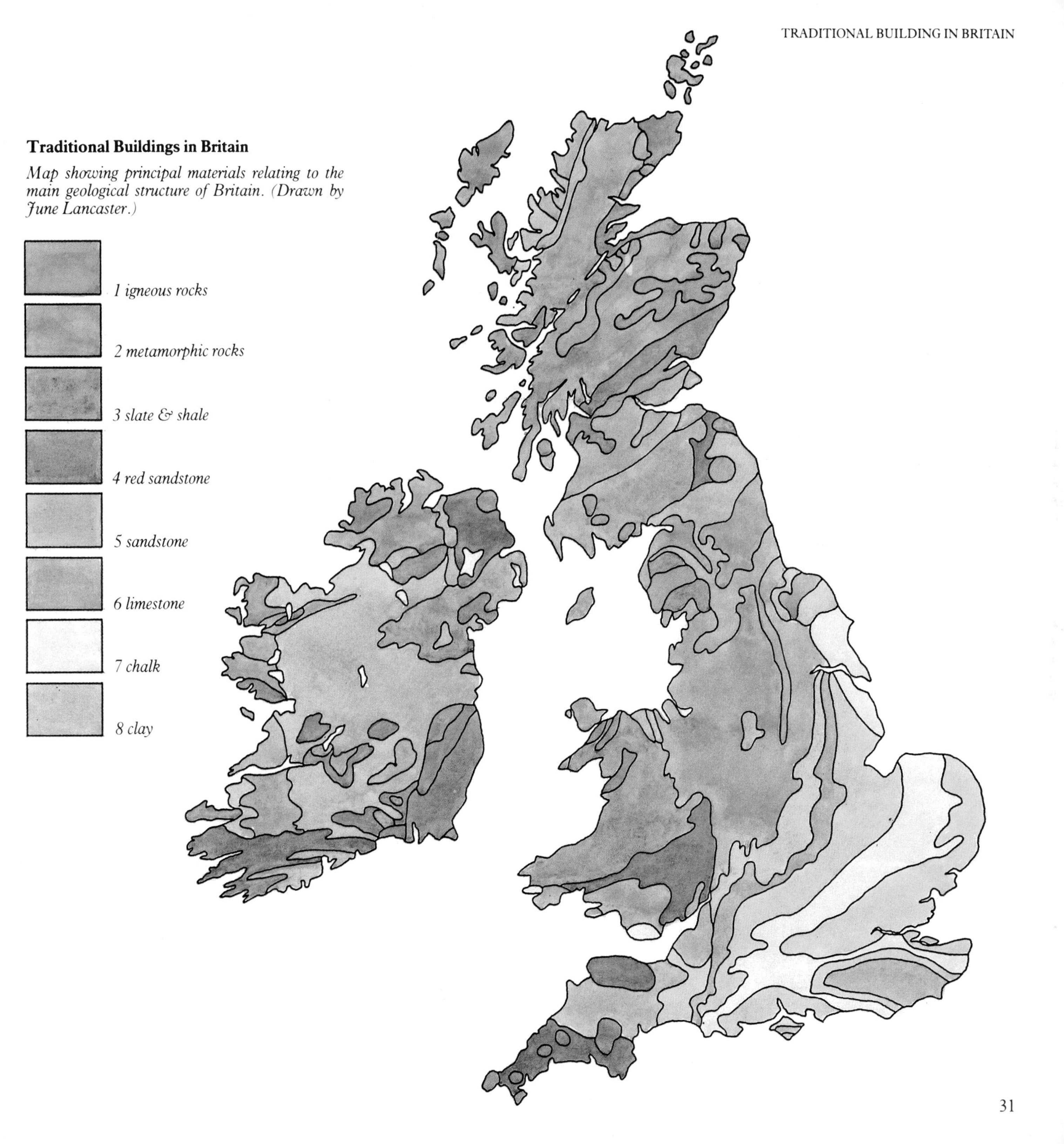

Traditional Buildings in Britain

Map showing principal materials relating to the main geological structure of Britain. (Drawn by June Lancaster.)

pressed or daubed onto a small frame of withies. But other materials such as cob, chalk lumps, wichert, stone, tiles and slate have all been used at various times, as well as lath and plaster. The main function of the material was for waterproofing and draught exclusion, and for both purposes some form of overall protective paint was desirable. This distemper, as it was called, was derived from lime, with additives such as milk, size, bull's blood, beer or tallow, for binding[7]. Its use is recorded as early as the twelfth century, when it was applied to some houses with good masonry, to some churches, and possibly castles.[8] 'Blue-black', a carbon made from vegetable matter, was sometimes added to make it appear less cold; this was displaced by Reckitts blue in the nineteenth century. Pigments such as 'rodel' or red ochre, and yellow ochre (of which Oxford ochre is the best known), pale green verdigris, and lime-blue (made from copper sulphate), were also used for colouring[9]. As to colour distribution there is much speculation but little firm evidence. Records are unreliable on descriptions of colours and there are few contemporary paintings of ordinary houses which constitute historical records. But traces of paint have been found in the roof spaces of some of the older houses and these indicate that, at least in some places, much stronger colours were previously used than is now the case. Pink and white are still commonly associated with Devon, pink and yellow with Suffolk, and white and cream, or yellow, appear to have had a universal application. The colour described as 'Suffolk Pink' is however red ochre, much more intense than the pastel pinks in current use[10].

The other common building materials, stone and brick, and their offshoots, can very broadly be related to the two main divisions of the country: the uplands and the lowlands. The Midlands, north and west are stone country, extending from the old hard rocks washed by the Atlantic to the eastern boundary of oolitic limestone that extends in a serpentine curve, like a backbone, from Dorset to Yorkshire. On it lie the quarries that have supplied our most celebrated building stones: Portland, Doulting, Bath, Painswick, Taynton, Weldon, Ketton, Barnack, Clipsham, Ancaster, Stonesfield and Collyweston[11]. These occur in a wide range of colours from the whites of Portland through the creams and yellows of Bath and Clipsham to a dark brown. To the north and west of this belt, the older geological formations also yield many qualities and colours of stone, from the red, yellow, brown and grey sandstones of the west Midlands, to the tough brown gritstones and carboniferous limestones of the north. Beyond them lie the shales and slates, which are green in the Lake District, brown in parts of Devon and Cornwall, and red and purple in north Wales mingled with the greys of the older harder rocks. Sometimes they give their colour directly to the soils. The red soils of Devon are due to the red sandstones of the Devonian period. They give colour also to the soils and many of the buildings in parts of Herefordshire and the Welsh Marches, Worcestershire and Monmouth, as well as parts of Scotland, Ireland and Wales. These and the marlstones of the Triassic are responsible for bands of red soils which run right across the country from Devon to Yorkshire, and westwards to the Lancashire coast. Others have a more tenuous relationship, their colour being picked up only in elements of the soil.

Stone, although readily available in many districts, was not a cheap material to work. It is heavy, and until the building of the canals and the railways, the cost of transport was restrictive. The accounts of the Hospital of Saint John at Sherborne (1438–1348) show the cost of carting lias stone twelve miles by road to be more than the cost of the stone itself.[12] An exception was made for the church, the only building dating as far back as the twelfth century, which was nearly always built of stone. Another important use was for castles and bridges, and the stone building tradition continued through manor houses (at first fortified) and the occasional public building, often combined with timber framing. But it was not until the seventeenth century, when timber became too expensive in certain areas, that the techniques of stone building were much used for ordinary houses. Then it was due less to the cheapness of labour or material (although stone was still cheaper than the more fire-resistant brick, which was at first used only for chimney stacks) than to the wealth of the merchants and farmers in the sheep-rearing areas of the country. Previously stone had been incorporated into the interstices of timber-framed buildings, or combined with mud or lime to make enormously thick walls. Some of these stones, gathered from the fields and the river-beds (called 'presents' in Cornwall) are very large[13]. The largest stones were used for corners and for framing doors and windows, and the areas in between filled in with more or less random rubble, which in some cases was plastered and painted white or colour-washed. In this way the 'framing' stones were emphasised, sometimes in their rough form, sometimes finely dressed, and sometimes themselves painted in contrast to the areas of infilling. Later, when stone became scarce, the pattern would be repeated in cement render. The working of stone depends either upon its softness or the degree to which it can be split. The extent to which it was worked depended on these two factors: its softness and the quality of the building. The improvement of stone-cutting techniques in the eighteenth and nineteenth centuries greatly widened the possibilities.

But it is brick, more than other material, that sets the tone for any colour study of buildings in Britain. Considering how useful it is, how easy to handle (each brick being a one-hand size), how flexible in building, how fire-resistant, how easy to make, and how beautiful it can be, it is surprising that it took us so long to develop. The Romans made large, thin brick tiles (12″ × 6″ × 1¼″ to 18″ × 12″ × 1½″) in faggot-fired open clamps[14]. Some of these were taken from the site of Verulamium by the Norman builders to build the tower of Saint Albans Abbey. But it is a rare example. Small Flemish bricks also began to be imported on the east coast, including a large consignment for the Tower of London in 1278, and there is some evidence of local industries. The first of any size was at Hull, which had trading connection with the Hanseatic towns. This led to the construction in brick of the large church of Holy Trinity between 1315 and 1345, the nave vault of Beverley Minster, and eventually, in the second half of the fourteenth century, to the rebuilding of the town of Hull in brick. Shortage of stone and abundant clays in the lowland areas of the country provided opportunities for itinerant brickmakers who would set up their clamps near the sites where buildings were required. At first the brick was confined almost wholly to important buildings, and until the end of the fifteenth century these were almost exclusively in the east of England, with very few south of the Thames. It was the Tudors who gave a boost to the industry with buildings such as Hampton Court and Saint James' Palace, which provided opportunities for ingenious ornamentation, and at the same time demonstrated the flexibility of the material. By the seventeenth century it had become fashionable at the vernacular level not only to build but to reface timber-framed buildings in brick, and to provide chimneys. The threat of fire, and particularly the Fire of London, provided further impetus. Almost overnight, London became a

Wooded hilltops, pasture slopes and settlements in the hollows express the character of the Herefordshire landscape seen from the Malvern Hills.

brick city[15].

The best bricks and tiles require two different clays: one plastic, the other sandy and non-plastic to counteract shrinkage. The colours depend upon the presence of different minerals, and the degree of firing. A high iron content, common in many parts of Britain, produces bright red bricks. The brownish bricks of Humberside contain little iron but plenty of lime (although the early bricks of Hull were red and blue); the yellow bricks of the Thames Valley contain chalk or sulphur; the whites of Sussex and East Anglia, and the greys of Oxfordshire, Berkshire and Hampshire, contain lime but no iron. The blacks of South Wales, Surrey, Sussex and Berkshire contain manganese[16].

A brick map would be highly complex because of the variety and the changes that have occurred through the mechanisation of the industry. It is nevertheless possible to identify certain clear local associations. In the Vale of York, for instance, the bricks are predominantly brown, in parts of Oxfordshire and Buckinghamshire they are purple and red, and in the Thames Valley red, yellow and white. In East Anglia they are again red, and in Surrey, Sussex and Kent are found the reddest of all red bricks and tiles. Here the walls are often tile-hung and the roofs unusually high-pitched, as though their builders could not resist such a splendid display of colour.

The roof is in fact one of the most noticeable parts of a building seen at a distance in the landscape; a fact which we may find disturbing in the 'white' asbestos farm extensions; or positively painful when contemplating the Victorian suburbs of Manchester and Birmingham. But it is also one of the most vulnerable parts; the first to decay and be replaced. For centuries thatch and stone tiles in stone districts were the commonest materials in use. But thatch was so vulnerable to fire that its use was prohibited in London as early 1212. It was made from a variety of materials including: flax, broom, sedge, straw and reed; Norfolk reed being the most durable, lasting for more than 60 years[17]. But all are vulnerable, even with the coating of lime that was sometimes used for protection, and it is a measure of the persistance of our traditions that so many have survived.

Sandstone and limestone tiles were common in stone districts, where they can still be seen in perfect harmony with the stone walls. But in many cases they have been replaced by the much lighter Welsh slate. Not only is it strong and durable, but it has the great advantage of being easy to split into very thin layers, which makes for roofs approximately one fifth the weight of the equivalent in stone. Moreover this enabled the slates to be laid at the much lower pitch of 22°–26°, making it possible for

1

2

3

the roofs to be hidden behind parapets, a quality which endeared the material to the Georgian architects and builders[18].

Clay tiles have much in common with bricks, which were used to shield them in the kiln. But their early use for roofing and tile-hanging was much more widespread than that of brick, leading by the 1830s to the development of important tile-producing industries on the Staffordshire and Shropshire canals. In spite of these there was little tiling in the north except on the east coast. Stone and slate were recognised as the materials appropriate to the uplands. Since then whole areas of Lancashire have disappeared under a rash of shiny pinkish red tiles and bricks; the infamous 'Accrington Bloods'. By contrast, the bright orange-red pantiles which distinguish the towns and villages of the east coast, have a rare beauty and appropriateness. The oldest were imported from Holland to ports all the way up from Suffolk to the Firth of Forth; later they were made in London and Somerset. Their dynamic shape and colour relates particularly well to the bright flint and colour-washed walls of the eastern seaboard[19].

The ways in which the colours of buildings contribute to the genius loci are many and varied. Sometimes the colour echoes that of the rock only; sometimes only of the soil. On the red sandstone there is a dramatic relationship of rocks and soils. In some cases the strongest links are vegetable, as in wood and thatch, ►

Many factors, including rocks, soils, vegetation, building materials and styles contribute to the genius loci. Sometimes their effects are dramatic in colouring whole areas; sometimes their influence is so subtle that it is easily overlooked.

1. *Lulworth Cove, Dorset. (Photograph by Roger Seijo)*

2. *Robin Hood's Bay on the Yorkshire coast.*

3. *Houses in the old trading port of Culross on the Forth, west of Edinburgh.*

4. *Flint gives a sparkling quality to the buildings of the chalk, particularly when contrasted with bright red brick as in this Norfolk example.*

5. *Houses at Dysart on the coast of Fife.*

6. *Yellow and grey predominate in the gravestones and buildings of the limestone town of Stamford.*

7. *Greys in the Cornish village of Porthleven.*

8. *Cotswold character expressed in open fields, beech trees and stone walling.*

9. *Brick has come to many areas, adding a strong element of redness to this Avebury cottage.*

4

5

6

7

8

9

1

2

3

which can be almost self-effacing. These are relationships of visual affinity. In others the links are more tenuous: the buildings acting as indicators of what lies unseen beneath the surface. All embody in their form, material and detail, centuries of hard-learned skills; and response to changing conditions. Local traditions of applied colour have also developed. The colour-wash traditions of Suffolk and the south-west are well-known, but the technique is applied in many other places. White-painted and black-stained weather-boarding belong to the south-east; and the traditions of painting buildings black and white are widespread. Seaside towns have their own vernacular of gaily coloured houses and shops.

Change, as we have seen, is a most significant factor in our vernacular traditions: it has occurred in the past because a cheaper or more practical way of doing things became available. Brick and slate are but two examples. Both are somewhat maligned by historical purists because they were not produced in many of the areas where they have been used. But what point in history should we choose? If we were able to go back 400 years we should see the Cotswolds as a country of wood and thatch. We can only judge by what we see now. Our judgement therefore cannot only be made on a historical basis. It must also be aesthetic, and in this colour plays an overriding part.

The traditions of course have been seriously assaulted by the industrial expansions of the nineteenth and twentieth centuries, particularly by the spread of brick and tile, which cause a dramatic change of colour to a district. Also they are further eroded by many present day developments. With the support of the Civic Trust, awards are given for: 'new buildings in the design of which respect has been paid to the character of neighbouring buildings and natural surroundings'. Only rarely can these new buildings be built of local materials, and never in precisely the traditional way. Their designers can however, by a careful study of their scale, form, detail and colour, achieve successful integration. The genius loci is a vulnerable quality, dependent upon the community, and it is easily disrupted. By understanding something of that quality, by seeing the subtle ways in which it is expressed; particularly in colour, we can help to preserve it; and more importantly, to create new places in which it can effectively develop.

1. *The smooth, expansive nature of the chalk landscape is enhanced by the elegance of the beech tree which here gives a reddish–purple bias to the scene. Wye, Kent.*

2. *Black and white 'magpie houses' give a special lightness to the Herefordshire town of Ledbury.*

3. *The dark brown gritstone walls are further darkened by soot in the Pennine landscape at Hebden Bridge, Yorkshire. (Photograph by Roger Seijo.)*

Weald and Downland

Red, in the south-east, is the colour given to the bricks and tiles. These are of such bright intensity as to make other red bricks look dull. But they owe their brilliance also to the lush green landscape against which many of them are seen. The colour derives from the high iron content of the Wealden soil, which also served a vigorous iron industry, powered by water and fuelled by charcoal from the abundant woodlands. So abundant were these, that the oak came to be called 'the Sussex weed'. Timber houses are common, but their frames are often hidden by tile-hanging; roofs tend to be steep in pitch and sweep low to the ground. In the Weald the colours change from a predominance of red to a

4

5

6

predominance of yellow, dark brown and black stone tinged with orange. On the chalk the colours change again, to the cooler and more reflective colours of flint, chalk and pale cream limestone – but still permeated with brick and tile. In places these are complemented by black 'mathematical tiles' hung on the façades. Flint is also blackened in Brighton, and the practice of blackening weather-boarding is widespread. The reds of brick and tile which are sometimes lightly tinged with blue work generally in a relationship of opposites with the greens of vegetation; the Wealden browns and yellows have a closer affinity, and the greys of the chalk act in a more neutral way.

4. *The smooth profile is characteristic of the chalk landscape. South Downs.*
5. *The yellow stone of this cottage at Amberley, Sussex, has a strong affinity with the surrounding colours.*
6. *The red bricks and tiles give maximum colour contrast to this cottage at Chiddingfold, Surrey.*

1

2

3

4

5

6

7

8

9

10

11

1. *Cottage at Amberley, Sussex.*

2. *Wealden house built of carstone, a black ironstone with orange veins.*

3. *Red houses in Petworth, Sussex.*

4. *Limestone brick and timber house near Witley with black weather-boarded barn.*

5. *Wealden cottage in carstone, Sussex.*

6. *Half-timbered inn with flint infill panels. In the shade the flint looks grey and cold. Near Amberley, Sussex.*

7. *When sunlit, the flint appears warm. Brick and flint house near Amberley, Sussex.*

8. *Wealden cottage in carstone, Sussex.*

9. *Black, common in weather-boarding and applied to some flint façades, is also a characteristic of 'mathematical' tiling, a very precise form of tile hanging which became increasingly fashionable after the imposition of the Brick Tax. Ditchling, Sussex. (Photograph by Tom Turner.)*

10. *Red tile-hanging at Petworth.*

11. *Farmhouse at Ditchling, Sussex, with 'mathematical' tiles. (Photograph by Tom Turner.)*

1

2

Suffolk

East Anglia is the most stoneless region of Britain. For this reason there has developed an early reliance upon the use of other materials, including flint, brick and mud, as well as timber, the basic building material of the country as a whole. Flint was used in the Middle Ages for building round church towers, which required no quoins, and later for facing rectangular buildings in combination with brick – used in Essex as early as the fifteenth century. Thatch and pantiles at first imported, were used for roofing. But timber-framed buildings are still a characteristic of many old towns and villages of Essex, Hertfordshire and Suffolk. Strangely it is, with certain exceptions, rather less for the timber frames than for the colour-wash that this area is celebrated. Covering over the frames with plaster was fashionable from the seventeenth century onwards, and by 1900 virtually every building in Lavenham had a coating of plaster. But originally the frames had been exposed, merely washed over with lime-wash in common with the infill panels. The traditional colours used in Suffolk were red and yellow ochre, the former being described as 'Suffolk pink'. This was much redder and more highly saturated than the colour now commonly used[1]*. Undoubtedly, fading and wear and tear produced a variety of different shades which no longer occur, due to the benefits of colour-fastness, weather-proofing and covering capacity of modern paints. Harmonic unity is more readily achieved with analagous colours than with contrasting ones. Therefore, in a general ambience of pinks and yellows, blues and greens – even though they were popular Georgian colours – look out of place. Blue, moreover, appears particularly intense when the light is poor.*

1. *Farm near Wickham Market.*

2. *Little Hall, Lavenham.*

3. *Debenham.*

4. *Kersey.*

5. *Hadleigh.*

6. *Cavendish.*

7. *Market Hall, Lavenham.*

8. *Aldeburgh.*

3

4

5

6

7

8

1

2

3

4

5

6

The Redlands

This was the Devon name for the strikingly red soils that derive from the Devonian sandstone. Not only are they rich in colour, but they are associated with some of the best agricultural land in the country; land which was continuously fought over in Saxon times. These lush pastures extend through much of the West Midlands and the northwest where the red sandstones, often far from red, were an important building material. In Devon it was used in many different colours for the churches, which are noted for their tall towers, for the manor houses and in the form of rubble for farm buildings. But it is cob that is most typically associated with Devon and West Somerset. This is mud mixed with chopped straw, horse-hair, dung, some chalk, rubble and gravel. The resulting walls are some two feet thick, and because they are handmade, they are uneven, with rounded corners and irregular tops, perfectly matched with the undulating lines of thatch. Although the walls of some farm buildings are left unpainted, cottages are generally colour-washed, in white, cream and/or pink, sometimes with tarred plinths. These rounded forms and the colours associated with them seem to grow out of the landscape, which is one of the most intimate and seductive in the country. The applied colours: black, white, cream, pink, are echoed in the rocks: red sandstone, yellow greensand, white chalk and grey flint, all of which in turn find their expression in stone buildings.

7

8

1, 2, 7, 8. *The small village of Sidbury lies in the characteristically deep valley cut into the greensand plateau by the river Sid. Most of the older cottages are of cob painted white or cream with black tarred plinths, and with roofs of thatch or its substitutes, slate or pantiles. Some of the Victorian cottages are of grey stone like the church which is unique for its Saxon crypt, and interesting for the mediaeval murals in yellow and red earth colours.*

3. *Branscombe straggles along the sides of two steep wooded valleys cut through the chalk and greensand to the softer red marl beneath. These 'rocks' can be seen in the cliffs where the stream flows into the sea. The cottages characteristically are derived from all three, being of stone, flint, and cob painted cream, white, or occasionally pink as in this example.*

4, 5, 6. *The colour of the Redlands is most evident in the soil and in the farm buildings which are directly derived from it. The multi-coloured stone, the mud walls and plaster and the rich earth seen here in the Exe valley, have a common colour affinity.*

1

2

3

Snowdonia

Snowdonia is the classic hunting ground for geologists. Whole series of rocks, from granite and the Pre-Cambrian gneisses, quartzes and schists, to the Cambrian slates and the Silurian limestones and shales are found in the area. But slate is the most synomymous with Snowdonia. Mountains bare their purplish bones to the sky, giving a dark heavy emphasis to the landscape. The great durability of the material, combined with the ease with which it can be split, makes it ideal for building. There are areas around the quarries where almost everything is built of slate: walls, roofs, floors, porches, and even beams. Also it was used for those curious slate-slab fences threaded with wire. Slate occurs in several colours: black, grey, green, blue, red, purple – all of which are basically darker than the vegetation. The colours of most natural materials, by contrast, are lighter, and in the case of red brick and tiles, more intense. But in the mountain areas of Wales all colours are intensified by the frequency of mist and rain: the grass is greener, the dead bracken more orange, and even the slate glows with a sombre intensity. To these are added the black, white and greys of quartz and granite, and the greens and browns of the other rocks.

1. *The white walls make it easy to see this farmhouse from a distance; an important factor in isolated areas. Slate is used for everything possible, including fencing. Llanberis.*

2. *Slate has many colours, several of which are seen in these buildings near Bethesda.*

3. *Llanberis Pass.*

4. *Cottage at Dinorwic. A tradition of painting the stone joints has developed recently.*

4

1

2

3

4

1. *Pattern of old stone walls in the area of igneous rocks near Llanberis.*

2. *House near Bethesda.*

3. *House at Holyhead, Anglesey.*

4. *Slate graves near Caernarvon.*

5

Berwick and the Lothians

Outcrops of purple-red volcanic rock and Old Red Sandstone give colour to the region north of Berwick-upon-Tweed. It is a wide, open landscape of large farms and fertile soils, including the coveted 'Dunbar red potato soil'. Its rich red is only surpassed by the brilliance of the sandstone cliffs of Redheuth. This material is used for quoins and for door and window jambs, where it stands in contrast against the more subdued colours of random rubble, rough-cast or pebbledash. The colour, when the stone is dry is often a warm pink, that is echoed in later houses by the use of brick for jambs. Harling, or rendering, is still practised using a mixture of lime and crushed seashells, giving a sparkling off-white finish; the Scots preferred to have houses that looked all of one piece, rather than broken up with fussy joints. Pebbledash is now common, but with careful margins left around openings for the addition of colour, perhaps yellow ochre. The colours of paintwork are variable, but with a frequency of black and white. Farm doors are occasionally red, or blue, but more often 'farmer's green'. Colour-wash plays an important part in the towns, where there is a bias towards the warmer hues: reds, yellows and browns, all trimmed in black and white, and a minimum of blue. Roofs are mostly of slate, but it is an area also of pantiles, the bright orange-red of which adds a piquant note to the deeper reds of this rich landscape.

5. *The moisture in this outcrop of Old Red Sandstone near Redheuth in Berwickshire increases its redness.*

6. *The red sandstone of this boundary pillar is an indicator of the unseen rocks below. Redheuth.*

6

1

3

4

2

1. *Harbour at St Abbs.*

2. *The pinkish-red igneous rocks dominate the area of the pier. St Abbs.*

3. *Rocks at St Abbs.*

4. *Fisherman's store, St Abbs.*

5. *Rendered and painted houses in Dunbar.*

6. *Closely related colours on houses in Dunbar.*

7. *Fisherman's store, St Abbs.*

8. *Red sandstone used for framing a doorway decoratively. Barn at Redheugh.*

9. *The opposite qualities of the blue door and red stone serve to emphasise their respective colours. St Abbs.*

10. *'Dunbar red potato soil'. Dunbar, Lothian.*

CARCARE
Lothian Printers
Antiques

5

HEN&CHICKE

6

POST OFFICE
LICENCED
GROCER
NO PARKING
BEYOND
THIS POINT

7

8

9

10

Colour and the countryside

Earth, rock, water, plants, and buildings: these are the materials which give the landscape its own special character. Colours reflected from their many surfaces can no longer be simple Like the patches of colour in pointillist paintings they combine to create a variety of different images. From the middle distance at which we normally view the landscape, the colours of stones merge with those of the earth, those of the earth with the colours of crops, verges with hedges and hedgerows with trees. Buildings alone stand out. In the far distance the colours change again: all are combined into a general atmosphere of colour.

The insubstantial nature of colour is further demonstrated by weather, the effects of which, in the landscape, are most immediately apparent. Light occurs as either direct sunlight or reflected skylight. The proportions vary according to the location, the season, the time of day and the weather. The average intensity increases from winter to summer, and from the poles to the equator. Where the air is clear, as in high mountainous regions, the light is bright and clear; where it is dust or moisture-laden the light is more often diffused: a characteristic of temperate and forested regions, and increasingly of our dusty industrial cities. The light in Britain and other northern European countries is predominantly diffused. Humidity in the atmosphere casts a veil over everything, but it also acts in another way, moistening the surfaces of materials which, being smoothed by a film of water, no longer scatter the light, but reflect their own colour more intensely. This is particularly noticeable on a wet winter day when we see red brickwork contrasted with wet green grass: each colour stresses the intensity of the other. The green moreover, is likely to look bluish on account of cloud in the overcast sky scattering the blue wavelengths of light.[1]

Cloud, like mist and fog, is an essential characteristic of the changing landscape of Britain. Its presence provides constant variety, both in the backdrop of the sky and, when the sun is high, in the shadows cast upon the ground. The water droplets and dust particles combine to form clouds in many different patterns and formations, according to the relative positions of the observer and the sun. In the great cumulus clouds which are a common feature of our skies the water droplets are so close together as to render the clouds almost opaque, causing them to reflect a dazzling white light from the sun. But the shadowed undersides are grey, which become darker as they mass overhead. Sometimes in brilliant sunshine after a storm when the clouds are too thin to cast shadows on one another, the grey grows darker and darker until it becomes blue-black just before the cloud disappears. This is produced by the combination of the blackness of the clouds with the blue sky. Distant dark cumulus clouds also often look bluish because of the scattering effect of the blue light rays; the further they are away the more their colour approximates to the colour of the sky. By contrast bright clouds near to the horizon appear yellowish[2].

Another effect of the scattering of blue lig't wavelengths is the blue haze of distance, long familiar to painters, and described by Leonardo da Vinci as *aerial perspective*. The presence of dust and moisture particles in the atmosphere between us and the object viewed scatters the light rays which are superimposed upon the background, making it appear more uniform and more blue. Short wavelengths scatter most and long wavelengths scatter least; the reason also why the sky is blue. The scattering of blue light has also the effect of making distant bright objects appear redder. Mist or haze reduces the blueness and changes it to grey. Sometimes at intervals of high pressure when the air is very pure and transparent, as it often is between two showers of rain, the colours and shadows in the foreground become very distinct, and the dark parts of the background turn to purplish-blue[3]. Weather, or the atmosphere it creates, gives subtle expression to regional character. Many painters have been attracted by the clear light of the Atlantic; Monet liked the London fog, and Turner the mists of the mountains. On a less dramatic level we can see local differences which are links in the subtle chain of relationships between geology, topography, soils and plants.

Agriculture, is at the same time both the product and the determinant of the landscape pattern. The slow painstaking efforts of farmers and landowners have combined over the centuries to convert a land that was once forest into what is now virtually all farmland. Its basic character, that of upland or lowland, broadly corresponds to the two main geographical divisions of the country. Topographically there may be a difference of 500 feet: for example between the uplands of mid-Wales and the fertile flatlands of Essex. Climatically Powys receives an averge annual rainfall of 75 inches, three times that of Essex. The pattern is reflected in agriculture. Arable crops predominate in the east; pasture in the west.[4] While pasture is likely to remain green all through the ►

1

1. *Aerial perspective. Painters use this expression to describe the layers of blue haze with which dark surfaces are veiled, as seen in successive layers receding into the distance. It is caused by dust and moisture particles in the atmosphere between us and the object viewed, scattering the light rays which are superimposed upon the background, making it appear more uniform and more blue. The blueness, like the blueness of the sky, is due to the fact that the short wavelengths scatter most, and the long wavelengths least, making distant bright objects appear redder. Roussillon, Pyrenees.*

2. *Stormy sky over the Cotswolds. At intervals of high pressure between two showers of rain, when the air is pure and transparent, distant objects become very clear. The white farmhouse is seen at its brightest, and sunlight highlights the crests of the ploughland, turning it orange in contrast to the purplish blue sky.*

2

1

2

3

4

5

1. *Snow. Sufficient long wavelengths are penetrating the cloud cover to reflect the greens and browns of the vegetation which are modified by the whiteness of the snow on the ground. This gives unity to all the colours. North Wales.*

2. *Snow, London. Contrast is increased by the heavily overcast sky, which limits the penetration of the warm wavelengths of light.*

3. *Rain, mist and cloud are merged into an atmosphere of grey. Scotland.*

4. *White cumulus cloud adds another dimension, dividing the landscape into three layers of background colour. Oxfordshire.*

5. *Mist flattens objects, making them appear like flat planes of stage scenery.*

year (but varying according to the nature of the grass and the animals grazing), arable lands may change three times: from the largely mineral colour of the bare earth, through the greens of growth to the yellow-golden ripeness of cereal crops. Others become a brighter yellow with mustard or rape, or, rarely, blue with cabbages or lavender flowers. These, like the invasive poppies, give a temporary colour emphasis to the landscape, but green is ever-present in the grass verges, and in trees and hedgerows in summer. In the uplands and on heaths the green is frequently dominated by heather and bracken which give strong autumn and winter colours. Everywhere in spring the vegetation greens are bright and intense. In summer they become duller, shifting as the year advances towards yellow and yellow-red which are again often bright and intense[5]. In winter the impact of green vegetation is at a minimum except for the greens of grass and winter crops, which are sometimes surprisingly bright. Winter in many arable areas shows a dominance of browns and blacks, enlivened by the crimsons and yellows of swelling buds. Many writers have commented on the qualities of green in the English landscape. Adrian Stokes compares 'the bright lifting colour of the ground where grass covers it' (in England), to that of Italy 'in whose bright landscape there is a prevalence of neutral colours that gain from each other'[6]. It is a sentiment that might be echoed by many painters and photographers, and landscape designers. Perhaps it was not only for proprietorial reasons that Capability Brown and his eighteenth-century patrons encircled their estates with perimeter woodlands. Goethe found green to be the colour emotionally restful and of easy focus but 'not an ideal colour for landscape background, because the eye is always seeking opportunities to limit its spread and define a boundary'[7]. One reason might well be the flat bluish quality that it assumes under an overcast sky; another, the relative lack of shadow when grazed or mown. Meadow grass, when allowed to grow long and mingle with wild flowers, never looks so uniformly green.

Trees invest the landscape with their own character, emphasising topography and indicating differences of soil and moisture. The southern lowlands once characterised by elm, are now represented by oak, hazel and field maple. The winding rivers are lined with alders, willows and poplars. The chalk downs are the country of beech and yew, sometimes accompanied by whitebeam and ash, which is seen at its best on limestone hillsides. Birch and oak are the trees of the sandy heathlands; also of the mountains, where they are accompanied by rowan, pine and larch. Each has its own character and its own colours. Several species, like the hawthorn, grow virtually anywhere, but they never grow in the same way.

When we look across a field we become aware of diminishing texture. The details of earth, stones and plants which we can see at close range become less evident as the distance increases, until they cannot be seen separately, and their colours merge with one another[8]. The effect can be observed in all uniform surfaces as well as in regularly arranged patterns or groups of objects of similar material. Thus we can see it in paving joints in perspective, in the numerous surfaces of the land, and on the surface of the sea.

The effects upon colour are very variable depending upon the nature and direction of the light and the alignment, texture and material of the surface. The sea for example tends to look darker towards the horizon because our view is directed towards the sloping surfaces of the waves[9]. Similarly, the crests and troughs of earth and vegetation surfaces will have a direct relationship with the angles of vision and consequently the colour seen. The colours of stones upon the surface of an arable field may become more evident as the distance increases because of their position in the line of vision, but that colour will be divorced from the object. As the distance increases we see colour as colour disembodied, filmy and insubstantial. Only as we approach and the details become clear is there a regression towards the real object and we no longer see it as separate from the material[10]. This is well illustrated by a patch of red at a distance, which on closer inspection appears as a wall which may be brick or stone or colour wash; it is only when we are close enough to see the detail of the joints that we know. If the wall is of brick or stone, the colour which we first see is a visual mixture of the material and the joints. In this way different coloured mortars can be used to give different overall colour appearance to the same material. Also the individual colours of earth and stones, leaves of grass and crops, and leaves and branches of trees, become visually mixed with one another, and with their shadows, as the distance increases. Their shadows, moreover, have colour.

The three-dimensional or vertical elements in the landscape relate to the texture gradient in a different way. These, in the form of walls and buildings are likely to appear as flat planes, each of more or less even texture, when seen at right angles or normal to the line of vision. Their texture is seen to diminish only when they are viewed in perspective. Hedges and trees will also appear progressively as flat planes of increasingly fine texture and light colour[11]. It is an effect dramatised when fog intervenes between the planes, but it is commonly seen at all times in our hazy atmosphere. Hills also seem foreshortened, appearing like the flat planes of stage scenery, revealing their relative distance only by the bands of colour. These bands, seen together, appear successively to darken from edge to edge. But this is an illusion created by *simultaneous contrast*; it is seen also in the apparent lightening of an even sky colour against the dark profile of roofs in the evening[12].

A tree seen in sunlight at close range exhibits colour in a variety of different ways. Direct sunlight falling upon the upper surfaces of the leaves will be reflected from them at different angles, transmitting different colours. These will vary from almost white, or glittering in the case of shiny leaves, to the most saturated green of the leaf. Some of the light will come through the leaves, giving a pale green or yellowish effect, and some will pass between them throwing a series of elliptical patches of sunlight on the ground.[13] In addition all of these surfaces as well as the different coloured surfaces of twigs and buds will cast reflections and shadows of different colours upon the adjoining surfaces, presenting a multi-coloured but co-ordinated picture. As we move away the textures appear to diminish and the colours to merge, producing an insubstantial effect of movement, which is compounded by the actual movement of the leaves and branches. Further away still, the colours become simpler, continuing to merge until they are indistinguishable from one another. Anders Hard observed in a measured experiment in Sweden, that the leaves which at close quarters appeared as a fairly strong yellowish-green, looked first blackish-green, then bluish-green, but with decreasing intensity as the observer moved away. At a distance of approximately one mile, the colour had become a whitish-grey, grading away to a reddish-blue at ten miles distance[14].

The interdependence of scale, form, texture and colour can be judged from an examination of the leaves themselves. Seen at the same distance, large leaves reflect more directly, small leaves more diffusely. The overall texture of the former, given by size, shape, distri-►

1

2

3

4

5

6

7

8

1. *Hill landscape, Black Mountains, Wales. The brownish red of dead bracken blends in closely related harmony with the yellows of stubble and dead grasses, and green is reduced to a minimum. As the shadows also are coloured, each colour area appears in different shades of greyness, in the lightly shaded foreground, in the sunny middle-ground and the darker shaded background.*

2. *Autumn, North Downs. The intensity of the reds, browns and yellow of autumn brings an exciting contrast to the green landscape.*

3. *Autumn, Richmond Park, London. The warm yellow of the low sun strengthens the relationship between the brown of the oaks, the red of the bracken, and the yellow of dead grass.*

4. *Crop colours. The strident yellow of oil seed rape is becoming a common feature on our countryside. Its high reflectivity has the effect of 'lightening' the landscape.*

5. *Cabbages and lavender flowers are unusual in contributing a blue colour to the landscape. Shadow accentuates the blueness.*

Texture gradient

6. *Close-to we can distinguish the separate colours of cabbage leaves, their shadows and the earth between them. In the distant view all these colours merge into a uniform but darker green. It can be seen here to be slightly more light-reflective than the adjacent brown earth, but much less so than the yellow of corn. Fife, Scotland.*

7. *Petworth, Sussex. The hill formed by Capability Brown from digging the lake is brighter and yellower towards its edge because we see a greater concentration of sunlit grasses than in the foreground where more green is visible. This helps us to see its 'roundness'.*

8. *Snowdonia. The various colours of stones and their shadows are mingled to form a uniform colour in the middle distance. But we often see the wall as grey. Here its colour is linked with that of the mountain tops as they are touched by the sun.*

1

2

3

4

bution, surface and shadows, is likely to be coarser than the latter. Shiny leaves reflect like mirrors while matt ones reflect dully. The fine hair on young leaves and on the undersides of certain species such as white willows and some poplars has an effect similar to that of the powdery bloom on grapes, diffusing the light. The effect is diversified by the differences between the upper and lower surfaces, and by the ways in which the leaves hang. Some like oak and holly are fixed stiffly to their branches; some like willow and birch are loosely suspended; and some like aspen and poplar have a nicked and rounded stalk section which makes them tremble at the slightest breeze. All these factors contribute to the visual texture and thus to the colour.

Water has its own special qualities, capable, on the one hand of reflecting the sky; on the other, of appearing a variety of different colours, depending upon the quality of the water and the reflections from the banks. In general blue lakes contain the purest water, the colour being due to the absorption of the orange and red rays of the spectrum. The commoner colours of green, yellow-green and yellow-brown are due to an increasing proportion of iron salts and humic acids as well as the scattering of brown-coloured particles. The presence of algae, vegetation and other suspended matter also has an effect. Under favourable conditions the greenness of water falling over a waterfall can be observed, and with it the effects of *simultaneous contrast:* the normally grey or black rocks appearing distinctly reddish[15].

The colours of the sea are more complex. In

1. *Similarity of hue: contrast of value. The yellow sunlight unites the winter greys, beiges and browns in a harmony of closely related colours. Cotswolds.*

2. *Birch wood, Epping Forest. The highly reflective trunks of birch trees appear thicker and provide strong contrast even when the light is poor.*

3. *Beechwood, Chilterns. The sunlight yellows the green lichens on the beech trunks, reducing the contrast and linking their colour more strongly with the red-brown ground cover.*

4. *Dering Wood, Kent. Colour in the woodland comprises variations of direct, transmitted and reflected light related to the surfaces of the leaves of different trees, shrubs, herbs and ground covers; – dead vegetation and bare earth, and in this case, water.*

5

6

5. *Reflections from wet beach. When it is very still, water becomes a mirror to the sky, making the beach blue, and here reflecting white clouds. North Wales.*

6. *The sea darkens towards the horizon because of the angle at which we see the waves against the light.*

general reflection is the predominant factor, but because of the interminable movement of the water, this occurs in many different ways. Firstly, all reflections are shifted towards the horizon because we look at the sloping surfaces of the waves: the colour often therefore appears darker than the sky immediately above the horizon. Secondly, the sea has a colour of its own, given by the combined effect of light scattering and absorption. If the light were only scattered the sea would appear milky white; if only absorbed it would appear black. In fact the combined effects work differently in different seas. The colours noted by one observer ranged from ultramarine towards the equator, through indigo, to olive green to the north. But the precise reason for the greenish colour of the North Sea, whether it be due to floating particles, diatoms, or other causes, has not been discovered[16].

Colour and Forestry[17]

Forestry provides a rare opportunity for landscape design with colour on a large scale. While it is true that the main purpose of forestry is and must be functional, to provide a timber crop; the current 10 per cent proportion of cost which is allowed for amenity value permits considerable scope for subtle detail. Also we should not forget that the natural climax vegetation of the British Isles is forest, and a balance of forest, woodland and open agricultural land may be regarded as acceptable and desirable.

The principal objections to large scale forestry are twofold. Firstly the conversion of open land such as hill pasture and moorland to forest, to some extent spoils them for recreational use and, secondly, the planting of large scale areas of unrelieved dark green conifers reduces visual interest. The answers to both objections can be made in terms of economics; but both should also be considered very carefully in terms of the landscape itself. Much of our landscape particularly in the south and west, is small scale and diverse in form and colour. But the landscape of the north of England and much of Scotland is of large scale and can accommodate a larger pattern of forests. Moreover as a natural habitat for our native conifers it is more sympathetic to the commercial spruces and firs.

Where the landscape is of intermediate scale, characterised by hills and open valleys, as in parts of Peebleshire and Kirkcudbright, the

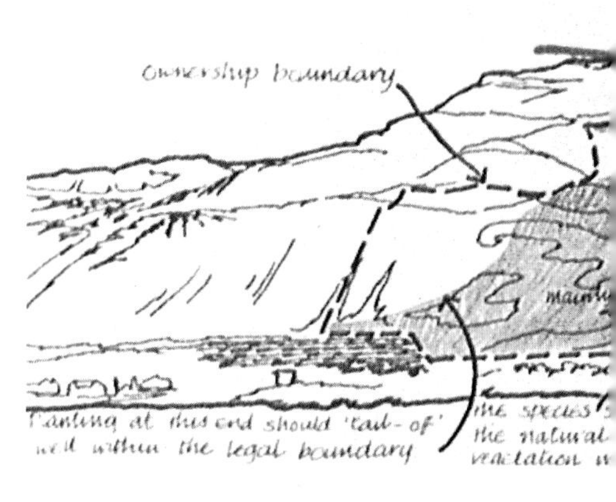

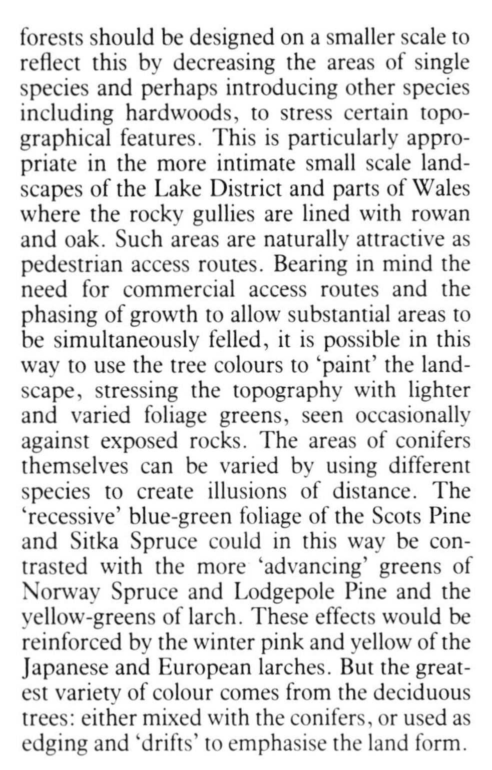

forests should be designed on a smaller scale to reflect this by decreasing the areas of single species and perhaps introducing other species including hardwoods, to stress certain topographical features. This is particularly appropriate in the more intimate small scale landscapes of the Lake District and parts of Wales where the rocky gullies are lined with rowan and oak. Such areas are naturally attractive as pedestrian access routes. Bearing in mind the need for commercial access routes and the phasing of growth to allow substantial areas to be simultaneously felled, it is possible in this way to use the tree colours to 'paint' the landscape, stressing the topography with lighter and varied foliage greens, seen occasionally against exposed rocks. The areas of conifers themselves can be varied by using different species to create illusions of distance. The 'recessive' blue-green foliage of the Scots Pine and Sitka Spruce could in this way be contrasted with the more 'advancing' greens of Norway Spruce and Lodgepole Pine and the yellow-greens of larch. These effects would be reinforced by the winter pink and yellow of the Japanese and European larches. But the greatest variety of colour comes from the deciduous trees: either mixed with the conifers, or used as edging and 'drifts' to emphasise the land form.

1. *The low spreading Cheviot Hills can accommodate large scale coniferous forests. But the dark greens of the forest should be used to reinforce the land form of hills as seen here in the distance; not broken into sharp rectangles as in the foreground. Redesdale Forest, Northumberland.*

Design for a forest

2. *Working with the Forestry Commission, within the constraints imposed by soils, climate and forestry management, the landscape architect sought to enhance the undramatic face of Beinn Ghuilean by 'painting' with trees. The bulk of the planting is deciduous larch which is used to highlight the slopes rising up from the 'heavy' base-planting of dark conifers. Some land is sacrificed at one end because of an awkwardly aligned legal boundary. At the other end of the forest is wrapped around to emphasise the slopes and to create the illusion of distance, but leaving the familiar skyline largely unaltered. Species include 84,000 larch, 58,000 Sitka spruce, 46,000 lodgepole pines, and 8,000 broad-leaved trees including: birch, alder, oak, rowan, ash and wild cherry. (Design and photographs by Clifford Tandy of Land Use Consultants in association with the Forestry Commission)*

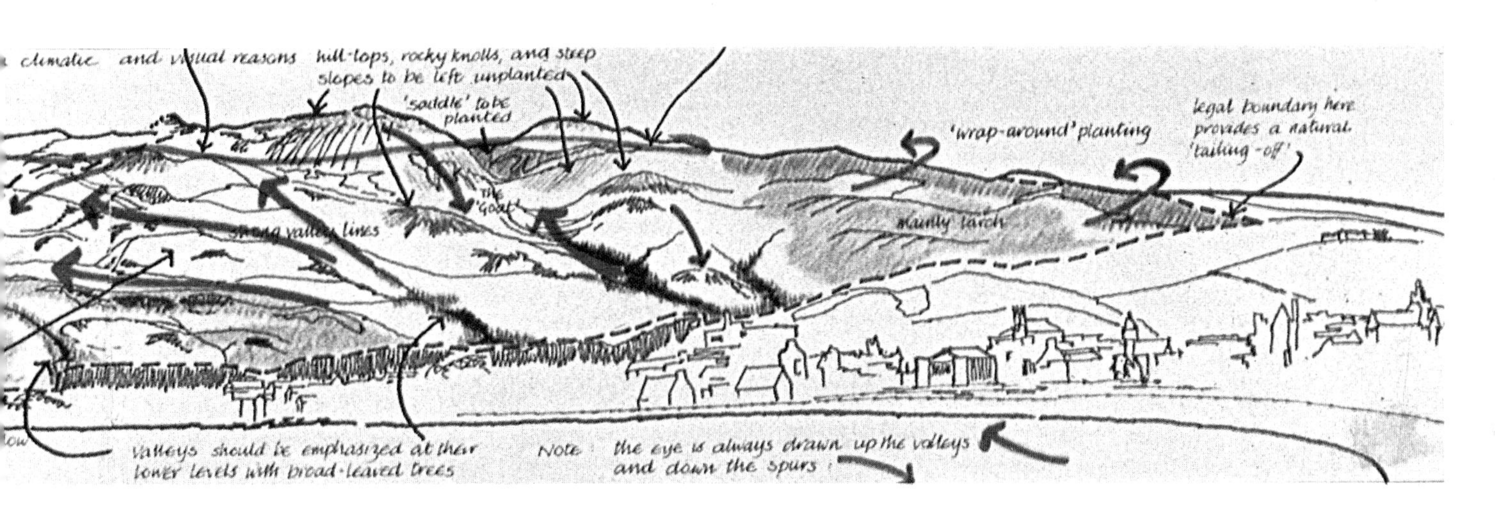
climatic and visual reasons
hill-tops, rocky knolls, and steep slopes to be left unplanted
'saddle' to be planted
the 'Goat'
strong valley lines
'wrap-around' planting
legal boundary here provides a natural 'tailing-off'
mainly larch
valleys should be emphasized at their lower levels with broad-leaved trees
Note: the eye is always drawn up the valleys and down the spurs

1

3

2

4

1. *Forests are used to organise the landscape: hardwoods sheltering the farmlands in the valleys; conifers on the middle slopes. The relationship is good, but the bands of dark conifers could relate more sensitivity to the upper slopes. North Wales.*

2. *Although this landscape near Bala in central Wales is of a scale which can accommodate coniferous forest, some of these areas relate unsympathetically to the land form.*

3. *This beech forest in Kent echoes perfectly the undulations of the chalk land, with which the trees have an affinity of colour.*

4. *The traditional pattern and colours of farms and hardwood forest emphasise the topography. Central Wales.*

Colour and the Garden

Although horticulturalists and plant breeders have long been seeking to increase the size, number and intensity of flower colours (at least as far back as the sixteenth century with tulips), and nursery catalogues are packed with illustrations of single species, very few designers have come to terms with the way in which these colours should be used. William Robinson (1838–1935) and Gertrude Jekyll (1843–1932) are the best known. Robinson reacted violently against the rigid and heavy formality of Victorian gardens, exemplified in the work of Paxton and Kemp, particularly the practice of 'bedding out' of hothouse plants to provide a show of colour, which he distastefully called 'pastry-work gardening'. He advocated the use of English wild flowers, and the idea that the garden should 'grow out its site'[1]. The useful bedding out tradition is still, however, a century later, part of the stock-in-trade of our municipal parks departments, appearing as floral clocks up and down the country. Unfortunately, it is rarely used with any sense of colour coordination. Even in the German garden displays, where the designs are more adventurous, the colour schemes are often disturbingly garish.

The wild garden has on the other hand returned home, after being adopted by some of the more enterprising Swedish parks authorities in the 1950s and in Holland in the 1960s. As wild flower meadows disappear from our farms, we begin to create them in our parks. Both Robinson and Jekyll were attracted to cottage gardens, which were distinguished by their unpretentious mixture of vegetables, herbs and 'old-fashioned' flowers: all originally useful plants. Although displaying little if any deliberate concern for design or colour coordination, their apparent naturalness, based upon the limited use of a small number of hardy and thus appropriate plants, gave them a sense of belonging which could not contrast more strongly with the bedding out of bright hothouse plants which were chosen and bred to be long-lasting, consistent and predictable. Jekyll's approach was the more intellectual. During her training as an artist she was influenced by Turner, whose paintings she used to copy. In his principles of colour harmony, given in lectures on perspective to the Royal Academy, Turner had effectively reduced Newton's seven colour spectrum to the three pigment primaries: red, yellow and blue, believing them to be emblematic of the structure of the visible world in terms of their formal relationships and their physiological impact. 'Red was the most commanding colour, but the mediating colour in terms of tone; in aerial perspective red seems to be regarded as the colour of matter itself, yellow as the light (medium) and blue as the colour of distance'. The progression form red, through orange, yellow, and thence through white to blue is a sequence often used in his paintings, particularly in his later life when he was preoccupied with atmospheric light.

This was the sequence Jekyll used for the main border in her own garden at Munstead Wood which she developed as a kind of laboratory for much of her later work. She describes it as showing 'a distinct scheme of colour arrangement' running from 'a groundwork of grey and glaucous foliage' through 'flowers of pure blue, grey-blue, white, palest yellow and palest pink' and 'then passes through stronger yellows to orange and red' so that 'by the time the middle space of the border is reached the colour is strong and gorgeous'. It then 'recedes in an inverse sequence through orange and deep yellow to pale yellow, white and palest pink, again with blue-grey foliage', ending not with the pure blue hues but purples and lilacs. She summarises the effect: 'from a little way forward . . . the whole border can be seen as one picture, the cool colouring at the ends enhancing the brilliant warmth of the middle' so that after the eye has become 'saturated' with warm reds and yellows, the greys and blues will satisfy its 'strong appetite' for cool colours. Although she was much influenced by H. B. Brabazon, 'Britain's Lost Impressionist' (who may have introduced her to Chevreul's *The Principles of Harmony and Contrast of Colours*), there is no indication that Jekyll subscribed to the divisionist theory of colour which was adopted by many of the French Impressionits. That is the principle of mixing colours visually by placing small patches (or points in Pointillism) of spectral hues on the canvas instead of mixing them on the palette; a principle explored and expressed in the work of Seurat, Signac and Renoir. In fact she was wary of strong colours which she felt could scorch holes in a landscape, preferring such subtle shades as 'the pale silvery lavender, perhaps the loveliest colour of which a China Aster is capable'. Here she expresses both her preference, the acceptance of variability in the plant and in the effects of light. But she was not averse to the use of a touch of complementary colour to bring a planting scheme to life. In her proposal for 'Gardens of Special Colouring' she proposes a sequence of five compartments surrounded by

1

evergreen hedges, each devoted to a single colour theme: orange, grey, gold, blue and green. The grey garden, which also contains blue flowers, 'is seen at its best by reaching through the orange borders' because 'the strong rich colouring has the natural effect of making the eye eagerly desirous for the complementary colour . . . One never knew before how vividly bright *Ageratum* could be, or lavender or *Nepeta*[2].

Such intricacy of detail could scarcely survive (even if it had the degree of maintenance which Miss Jekyll's gardeners lavished on it); it is only in her writing and in the gardens of some devotees that the expression of her ideas can be seen. Sissinghurst, in particular the grey garden; Great Dixter; and Hestercombe are among them. None of Jekyll's passion for detail, which can in some measure be attributed to her short-sightedness; nor it seems, her boldness and inventiveness, appears to have been expressed in her paintings. Gardens and writing were her means of self-expression. Monet, by contrast, a near-contemporary, who shared Jekyll's love of gardens was essentially a painter, pre-occupied for much of his life with the problem of capturing the changing colours of light on canvas. His garden at Giverny can be seen as little more than a model for his paintings. The two skills have to some extent been combined in the work of the Brazilian, Roberto Burle-Marx (born 1909). Although highly skilled as a designer in many fields, he is chiefly known in Britain for the bold use of form and colour in his Brazilian gardens. These were in basically forest clearing characterised by the careful disposition of spatial elements in the form of tiled and sculptured walls, flowering trees, shrubs and in his early work, the striking use of serpentine swathes of ground cover plants in contrasting grey, purple, yellow and green. The choice of plants for their coloured foliage gives them the kind of permanence of a painting, or more precisely of a pile carpet, which is dependent upon light for its textural effects. Although the bright purple groundcover used by Burle-Marx would appear too bright in our soft light, there are many other ground covers which could be used more dramatically than merely to cover lawns and the bare earth between shrubs. Foliage guarantees a degree of permanence, unlike flowers, whose elusive qualities tax the most skilled designers. The best course, and the most appropriate, is, like Jekyll, to opt for a careful combination of both. In this, for guidance, we should look to nature.

Colour in nature is rarely intense over large areas. Concentrations of poppies, corn marigolds and bluebells only appear to coalesce when seen from a distance, and they are short-lived. Other intensely coloured flowers such as gentians and buttercups are muted by the mingled greens of their foliage, never seeming so brightly concentrated as the yellow crops of mustard and oil-seed rape. Also they are more usually scattered in drifts, relating to one another casually. The commonest colours in Britain are whites tinged with greens, pinks and yellows. They occur profusely in the flowers of many of our trees, and in wild flowers. Yellow is also common in wild flowers and in gorse and broom. But yellow, like the more intense red, is generally focussed in smaller areas than the white. Apart from poppies, which are exceptional, the brightest reds that we see are in the smaller flowers, in berries, and other ephemeral items such as fungi. Even the rose, famed for its redness, is in its natural wild form, only a gentle pink. The cult of colour has led us to select, breed and import a bewildering number and variety of plants, all of which are more or less favoured by our climate. We are faced with a choice of plants from every continent in the world, as well as home-bred exotics. In order to make that choice effectively we should recognise firstly the relative importance of the elements.

The garden is a microcosm of the landscape. As we 'read' the landscape by its trees and

1. *Hascombe Court. The garden for this Lutyens House may have been laid out by Gertrude Jekyll, and her influence can be seen in the planting, notably in the extensive use of grey foliaged plants such as lavender to provide a neutral background for the bright hues: in this case the red berries of cotoneaster horizontalis which blend well with the tiles of the house.*

2. *The White Garden, Sissinghaurst. Vita Sackville-West and Harold Nicholson used Jekyll's idea of the single colour garden for one of their enclosed gardens, and planted it only with green and grey-foliaged, and white flowering plants, creating a light reflective ambience. A similar principle was used in 'the Red Border' at Hidcote. (Photograph by Marian Thompson).*

2

1

2

3

4

1, 2. *Demonstration garden at Dartford, using a wide variety of herbaceous plants arranged according to scale, foliage texture and colour, and flower colour. (Designed by Marian Thompson for the Division of Landscape Architecture, Thames Polytechnic, Dartford.)*

3. *Variations on the theme of blue flowers with a touch of orange to enliven the effect. Sissinghurst.*

4. *This garden at Wakehurst Place has been planted in the manner of Gertrude Jekyll, using almost entirely pinks and purples. (Photograph by Marian Thompson.)*

5. *Contrasting flower colours. Blue against yellow.*

6. *Contrasting flower colours. Purple against yellow.*

7. *Painting with flowers. Burle-Marx used bright coloured foliage in Brazil. The purple and white flowers, foliage and even the dead heads of heather have been effectively used here in Kew Gardens.*

8. *Painting with flowers. This is relatively easy with bulbs of known colours. Usually there are far too many and they are far too mixed. Here some care has been taken to restrict the colours to analagous hues; only the white is intrusive. As the light fades there will be a 'colour shift' towards blue, the reds will appear blackish.*

9. *Contrast of greys and greens. The Tudor and Jacobean gardeners developed the use of herbs, arranging them in decorative parterres. Here in the reconstructed garden of Kew Palace the two greys of santolina and lavender are contrasted with the yellower green of box, seen against an enclosing hedge of the blackish-green yew.*

10. *Analagous harmonies seem to evoke an emotional response, especially when the warmest colours are used. Sissinghurst.*

hedgerows, walls and buildings, against the backgrounds of fields and hills, so we should be able to read the garden against the background of ground covers and enclosing hedges and walls. The trees and shrubs within should be arranged to organise and divide the space. They should moreover, be arranged in order of significance against the background, according to their scale, their form and texture, and their colour. The several types of colour contrast can be exploited in many different ways. These may vary from simple light-dark contrasts of object and background to the more complex contrasting relationships of hue. They may be►

5
6
7
8
9
10

concerned simply with the contrast of foliage as between greys and greens, or yellows and greens; but they will change constantly with the light.

Autumn colour may also bring change, and in winter the scene will be transformed. Flowers, depending upon their profusion and duration will also have a more or less dramatic effect, which may be either general or local. Autumn colour may be used to reverse the effects, temporarily turning the background to red or yellow, or this effect may be made permanent by using dark or heavy incidents against a light background. Gertrude Jekyll preferred backgrounds of grey or yellow-green contrasted with the dark green of yew to the bright characteristic mid-green of much of our native foliage, which she felt demanded a scale larger than that of the garden. The neutral greys form restful backgrounds to the bright hues of flowers which are often garish against the brighter greens. We may however choose the occasional bright contrast for dramatic effect, as indeed Jekyll did. But it is important that it should be controlled, not random. One writer proposed the exercise of designing a garden by moonlight when all colour is lost, to ensure that the forms are right[3]. The colour can then be introduced according to a limited palette. Hackett suggests using eccentric colour circles to give scope to the large numbers of flowers in particular hue regions. In this way yellow, which occupies only a small part of the average colour circles could be widened with orange, red and purple[4].

It is however by no means simple, either to co-ordinate growth-rates, flowering times and colour sequences; or for that matter to match flowers with colour-charts. Bedding-out with ready-made colours is the easy answer; using foliage plants only is a little more difficult; achieving colour harmonies with both flowers and foliage is approaching perfection.

1. *Contrasts of scale, enclosure, light and shade, pattern, texture and colour. Garden entrance in Barnes, London.*

2. *Harmony of analogy: wallflowers provide a good opportunity for analagous harmonies of reds, oranges and yellows which relate well to the surroundings, echoing the warm colours of most of our buildings.*

2

3

4

5

3. *Bedding-out is usually poorly sited and poorly designed, using unsympathetic colours. This rare example at Saint Fagans Folk Museum, Cardiff, is well placed on a bank between hedges, suitably restricted, simply designed using analagous reds, oranges and yellows, and it is appropriately seen across an informal herb garden.*

4. *Green on green. Greens are difficult to use on a small scale. But given space, as here in Lord Aberconway's garden at Bodnant, it is possible to use the light to exploit the many possible variations of this ubiquitous colour.*

5. *The blueness of bluebells is best seen in dim light or shadow. In bright sunlight they appear purplish. (Photograph by Marian Thompson.)*

Colour in towns and cities

The image of a city is strongly influenced by colour. We may think of Paris as grey, Amsterdam as red, and London a patchwork of red, white, yellow and black. These are the background colours against which the play of city life is enacted: the bright colours of the shops, the people, the buses and the advertisements. They are the colours by which we can identify a place and which help us to read the visual map of the city. In London the differences are extreme, between the cream and white buildings of Regents Park and Belgravia, the red of Knightsbridge, and the greys and yellows of West Kensington. Moving from one to the other is like experiencing a change of climate. The colours of the buildings themselves are subject to change; not only due to the light, but to renovation and replacement. Nevertheless these differences are useful in orientation; they serve to reinforce the movement patterns of path and street, street and square, as well as the over-riding traffic systems, which are fundamental to our cities. The part which colour plays in such developments is very variable. At the large scale it is usually more a product of the materials than of any conscious policy; at the pedestrain level it is likely to be at the whim of landlord, shopkeeper or local authority; at its most explicit, it takes the form of a profusion of signs. Attempts to co-ordinate these elements into a visual order by means of colour have been surprisingly rare. One such attempt was made at Turin in 1800.

In order to define the processional routes into the city a Council of Builders was commissioned to develop a system of 'chromatic pathways' leading via a network of streets and squares to Turin's centre, the Piazza Castello. The scheme was based upon some 80 colours which were popular in the city, and implemented by the processing of applications for redecoration. The council survived until 1845, and the colours, albeit somewhat debased under the general description Turin Yellow, were much praised by visitors early in the twentieth century. The scheme was revived in 1978 by the municipality who employed a team of architects and colour consultants to undertake an elaborate programme of restoration based upon a colour map drawn from archives and surviving paint samples. About one thousand buildings a year are being redecorated according to the system, using predominantly yellow ochre as a principal 'framing' and 'background' colour for the main streets and squares, supplemented by a coordinated range of subsidiary colours: greys, browns, pale blue and purple[1].

A similar enterprise was undertaken by the architect Bruno Taut at Magdeburg in Germany in 1921. Newly appointed to the Board of Works, he set about transforming the drab streets of the industrial city as a matter of public concern. Beginning with the city hall, which was painted Bordeaux red with white and yellow ochre details, the chromatic movement swept through the centre of the city. Unfortunately the durability of the colours and the rendered surfaces on which they were painted proved inadequate to the enterprise, and his many critics were jubilant. Taut moved on to experiment with the use of colour in housing schemes around Berlin. 'By means of variation in colour intensity and brilliance,' he wrote, 'we can expand the space between the house-rows in certain directions and compress it in others. Thus one of the key principles behind the enclosed colour scheme is an optical widening of both streets and yards by means of relatively dark colours.'

By comparison with the grimy streets of many industrial cities – not to mention the cement greys which were common in Germany – Taut's achievement was revolutionary. As he wrote in 1925: 'Our age is beginning to find itself; its blood is flowing a little quicker than before, its face is growing young again and happy and its cheeks are flushed with joy. Colour is reborn'[2]

The danger inherent in both schemes is that of imposition: in the one case of 'fixing' a culture in evolution, like a museum-piece; in the other of imposing the municipal taste. The advantages are those of coherence, which is most evident in our few examples of Palladian planning, notably in Bath, Cheltenham, and the West End of London. Colour plays no more than a background part in all of these, being either that of stone in Bath, or stucco, the Regency version of stone in London, and a mixture in Cheltenham. Although all were speculative developments, built piecemeal, all recognise the importance of visual as well as physical unity. Now many of our towns and cities, while being ever more tightly tied together by roads, are in danger of falling apart because of a lack of attention to the problems of visual and spatial coherence. As new developments jostle one another for attention, the needs of the pedestrian (who is after all a co-owner of the city), expressed in an identifiable hierarchy of place and movement, become more remote.

The problem of the unity of the street is one

London. Sky, water, buildings and bridges are the key elements of the river landscape. In this view the City of London is unified by a predominance of light–reflective 'colours', stressed by the dark grey tower blocks behind Saint Pauls and the grey cloud. This whiteness permeates the whole of London as well as many other cities in Britain. It is most obvious in the weathered surfaces of Portland Stone which are thrown into contrast by the blackness of its sheltered surfaces; (seen here on the drum and cupola of Saint Pauls and many riverside buildings); but also in painted stucco, concrete, and the paintwork of bridges, ships, and the doors and windows of most buildings. This colour balance is vulnerable to change through new colours, such as that of the yellow building beyond the National Theatre. It is also liable to be upset by changes in large surfaces of paintwork, such as the bridges, which a design spokesman for the GLC said he would like to paint in 'ice-cream colours', a total irrelevance.

with which the Civic Trust has long been associated. Colour inevitably plays a prominent part; in their co-operative improvement schemes they have tried to reconcile the conflicting views of individual owners, and at the same time reflect the essential character of the area. In this they have recognised the importance of all the factors from the structure and materials of the buildings and their details: shop-fronts, fascias, signs and lettering, including access and traffic. Nor have they neglected economic viability, which is a crucial consideration in relation to run-down areas particularly in industrial cities. The value of such work is incalculable; the danger is that of developing too much of a 'house-style', especially in terms of colour, which could create its own character.

When it comes to overall colour character, new towns are invariably a disappointment. Perhaps inevitably they tend to err on the side of conservatism or 'good taste' in providing a background against which the more colourful developments of the city can take place. In the case of the French new town of Le Havre that background is so rigidly consistent in design and so uniformly neutral in its concrete colour that individuality is almost totally lost. As though to make up for this lack of colour, the designers of some of the new towns around Paris have gone to the other extreme, celebrating a revolution of colour which Bruno Taut would have welcomed. This is particularly striking in slab and tower blocks, where colour has been used to break up the monotony of large concrete surfaces. In the best, by such colourists as J.P. Lenclos, it has been used spatially: not merely to emphasise the sculptural quality of the architecture, but to organise the different surfaces of the architecture in space. In other examples, in many countries of the world, such uses of colour have degenerated to no more than pattern-making or the

1

responses too haphazard. The best that we usually manage to achieve is unity within a precinct, or an area so large as to constitute a district, like the Barbican or Byker in Newcastle, which then become new city landmarks. Our failure too often is in relating them to one another and to the surrounding fabric of the city. We also fail to allow adequate scope for self-expression, which is an essential aspect of life, especially in the city. This occurs spontaneously in street markets, and in an organised way, in such centres as Piccadilly Circus: it occurs also notably, in 'street art', in shopfronts and window decorations, and in individually decorated houses. Some of these, occupied by immigrants, exhibit striking new colour palettes in our citites. But such individual expression is absent from most large-scale developments, even if there is space for it. The sombre fortress-like character of many developments positively militates against it. The informal Byker, on the other hand, has a colourful side, where people can lean over the brightly painted balconies and wander among the more casual areas of plants and lower density housing behind the wall. Colour is only one of the many factors which contribute to the making of places, but it is more significant than at first may be realised.

creation of a sort of super street art.[3]

The British new towns, being a late development of the Garden City ideal, depend more upon landscape. Although they have very successfully absorbed and adapted some old town streets, their new streets and centres tend to be either colourless or garish. Co-ordinated colour policies are also lacking in the towns as a whole. Some have been implemented in a limited way, but the British sense of individual freedom of choice, combined with a want of assurance in the uses of colour, has not allowed them to be carried to any significant conclusion. The policies are generally limited to offering a range of materials and colours working within a specific town centre, conservation area, housing or industrial site. The north, central and south zones of Milton Keynes are in fact distinguished by the use of predominant bands of colour in housing, but these differences are not obviously related either to one another or to the city as whole. the image of the city is, or will be that of trees: an appropriate image for such a low-density development.

Among the British new towns, Peterlee is unique in projecting a specific colour image. This is due to the employment of Victor Passmore from 1954–1967. The move was prompted by some dissatisfaction with the dull impression created by some of the housing that had been built on the plateau to the north of the centre; to employ an artist for such work was quite unprecedented. Artists have been employed in many New Towns, but strictly for the 'art'. Passmore had the advantage of being able to see buildings more in terms of forms and surfaces expressing colour than as combinations of materials enclosing space. He changed the basic brick colour from red to neutral greys, flattened the roofs, and introduced white-framed and panelled curtain walls incorporating windows. The layouts of the various groups of houses were also loosened, so that they were no longer tied rigidly to the roads. Colour was used sparingly: panels of dark red, brown, beige and yellow ochre, all earth colours, linked by the colour of the brickwork. Although there were constructional failures due to the unconventional building methods, the visual effect is like that of a series of paintings: areas of colour working together in carefully balanced colour compositions[4]. Corbusier had, on a much smaller scale, sought such a solution for his houses at Pessac in 1926. 'I want to do something poetic,' he said, and painted adjacent wall surfaces different colours, thereby achieving the illusion of weightlessness[5].

To create such an image in the modern city as a whole is never so simple. Its growth is too much subject to commercial pressures, the time scale too unpredictable, and individual

Colour, as all advertisers know, is a potent weapon. It is no accident that the house colours of the principal oil companies are primaries: it is however accidental that so many are seen together. Although petrol stations are often well designed in themselves they give the impression of having been conceived for more spacious places than are found in most of our towns and villages. The strong colour used to emphasise their horizontal lines contrasts unhappily with the small-scale vertical emphasis of traditional streets. When seen in juxtaposition with other strong colours this has a disturbing effect.

Large stores and supermarkets present a similar problem when they are fitted into the traditional street pattern, creating disturbance as much by their window stickers and other eye-catching ephemera as by unsympathetic design. Such profusion of display leads easily to the visual chaos which is an increasing source of confusion in our lives. Thence the eye seeks relief in calmer colours; in the neutral greys, browns, blacks and white, now more often associated with 'quality' shops; and in the simple message of the symbol, or its recent substitute, the logo.

In smaller shops colour often becomes iden-

2

3

4

5

1. *London. The winter light in London often has a pinkish quality which envelops sky, water, and concrete paving alike. The Houses of Parliament become part of a flat grey stage set against which the life of the river and the South Bank are enacted.*

Bridges

2–5. *Bridges have a unique character as vantage points between two territories, belonging neither to the one or the other. Apart from their historical significance in the city, their visual significance is twofold: as linking elements between the two territories, and as structures. Colour should be used in a way which recognises all three. A dark colour will stress the thinness of the cables in suspension bridges, compared with a light colour which exaggerates them. This is seen in the two pictures of the Albert Bridge showing different colour schemes* **2, 4**. *In one view the dominant 'whiteness' of the carriageway divorces it from the darker surfaces on either side. The beige panelling of the carriageway is eclipsed in this view by the brightness of its white surrounds. The overall effect is also marred by the almost matching beige chimneys of Battersea Power Station and the recently added central pier, which is structurally alien, has not quite successfully been 'painted out'. Of all the London Bridges, the colour scheme for Lambeth in black, brown, red, white and gold, has been most carefully designed to express the relationship between the structure and its historical origins, the buildings on either side, and red buses, symbolic of London life* **3, 5**. *(Design by Georgina Livingston.)*

tified with the wares, particularly evident in such traditional shops as tailors and herbalists, health food stores, and tea and coffee merchants, boutiques and perfumiers. Subtler advertisers have realised this and devised house colours which are appealing rather than demanding. Analagous colours; that is closely related hues arranged consecutively together, tend to have a calming effect, but they are rarely used in our environment. Advertisers have also been slow to take advantage of the optical possibilities of colour, as seen on the fascia of a South London optician, and in the advertisements for a well-known brand of cigarettes. The designer of the fascia has shown considerable wit and ingenuity in setting up a visual dialogue between blue and green planes

1

2

3

4

suggesting the shape of spectacles. The cigarette advertisements were more ambitious. These posters comprise squares of pure hues in varying degrees of lightness and intensity, juxtaposed, so that at a distance they form a picture, and seen close-to they become abstract patterns of colour. This was achieved by a process of computor graphics. Hues are arranged in various analagous and contrasting groups to give a variety of expressions of depth and movement, thus creating a vibrant 'moving' picture.

The brewery companies, traditionally wielding considerable influence over our environment, use different techniques. While most have a corporate image, some sell aggressively, giving unusual colour expression to their buildings; some sell sympathetically by allowing individual character in each building; and some others by uniformity. But the livery may change as the assumed needs for advertising change, giving different images to different pubs. Fortunately, even though we have lost many fine interiors, the buildings themselves are often interesting and important elements.

1. *The elegance and purity of form continues into Trafalgar Square, where the 'white' of Portland Stone is emphasised by the beiges and greys of sandstone and granite.*

2. *London is many colours. Moving from one part to the other is like experiencing a change of climate. The colours are more often a result of changes in architectural taste than of a conscious colour choice. The 'whiteness' of stucco which was all-embracing in the Regency Period has however permeated almost all subsequent building styles until recently in the form of colonnading, cornices, stone banding, porches and window reveals, or merely light painted windows and doors. Even when they are built in relatively dark stone the reflective quality of these lighter elements serves to lighten the effect of the darker buildings of brick. Prince Consort Road, Kensington, London.*

3, 4. *Regent Street and Piccadilly have lost most of their elegant buildings, but the lightness is retained, that of Piccadilly being emblazoned with advertisements. Their colour, both night and day, declares this to be the centre – 'the market place' – of London, although it is a traffic island.*

5

6

5. The unifying quality of 'whiteness' is apparent in John Nash's development of the West End of London, which extends from Regent's Park to Buckingham Palace. By diffused light the buildings assume a curiously two-dimensional quality, which disappears in strong sunlight. Chester Terrace, Regents Park, The Mall.

6. Cheltenham. The age of the spa came later to Cheltenham, which lacks the architectural purity of Bath. It is however unique in being unified by the Promenade, a tree-covered avenue which links the main parts of the town with the spa buildings. The stress here is more upon the pedestrian, on the sloping paved walk through trees with a background of stucco buildings lit from above. The relief of their columns and windows is highlighted against the painted background.

7, 8. The Georgian city of Bath, built between 1727–1781, depends entirely upon the architectural styles and the warm yellowish-brown stone for unity. The Royal Crescent, completes with a half ellipse the sequence of geometrical spaces which was begun with Queen's Square, extended up Gay Street to the Circus, and thence along John Street. Its curved form and its textured surface play with the light, reflecting it in a variety of different ways. The form also serves to 'embrace' the landscape which is separated by a concealed ha-ha. The interaction of town and countryside is carried further in Lansdowne Crescent, a transitional stage between the formal crescent and the informal terrace following a double serpentine curve which at the same time undulates with the landscape. The stone appears a weathered grey, providing a neutral background to the colour of grass and buttercups.

7

8

1, 2, 4. *Irregularity of scale, material and colour is more characteristically British than the Palladian uniformity, unity being achieved through the details of doors and windows. In Windsor, a town dominated by the grey-white limestone castle, the predominant material is brick, which occurs in several colours with a predominance of red. Coloured stucco is also common, occasionally concealing timber framing. This features prominantly in the Civic Trust co-operative improvement scheme.*

5

6

3. *The organisation and disposition of colour planes in the landscape. Peterlee, County Durham. Traditional English red-brick houses with pitched roofs, are often too strong a colour element in the green landscape to be used together in large numbers. While the single red-brick red-tiled building group can be an asset to the landscape; the multiplication of the type can be overpowering. This was appreciated by the painter Victor Passmore, when he was commissioned to participate in the design of housing for Peterlee New Town. He changed the brick colour from red to a neutral grey flattened the roofs, introduced white-framed and panelled curtain walls incorporating the windows and freed the houses from their rigid connection with the road system. Although there were constructional failures due to the unconventional building methods, the visual effect is like that of a painting.*

5, 6. *The 'Great Wall of Byker' in Newcastle combines two colour traditions in a totally contemporary way: that of English brickwork and the bright-stained woodwork traditions of Scandinavia* **5**. *The outside wall was designed to screen the proposed motorway; the inside, festooned with coloured balconies, to express the life of the people. Such gaiety is rare in Britain and often discouraged. This is particularly the case in the City of London's Barbican development, which was originally intended to reduce inner city decay by housing the workers* **6**. *The complex has developed into an unusually high quality precinct for the rich with very little scope for any spontaneous expression.*

7

7 and overleaf. *Spontaneous colour expression. The degree to which individuals can be allowed to express themselves has long preoccupied the guardians of our cities. Where such freedom is expressed either as simple painting or as street art, it can provide rewarding results. These can be seen decorating shops and houses scattered around our cities, often indicating the presence of immigrant communities who bring unfamiliar palettes of colours with them. Some of these are more or less pure expressions of their country of origin; others become assimilated and regurgitated as 'psychadelic' and 'pop' colour compositions.*

1

2

3

4

5

6

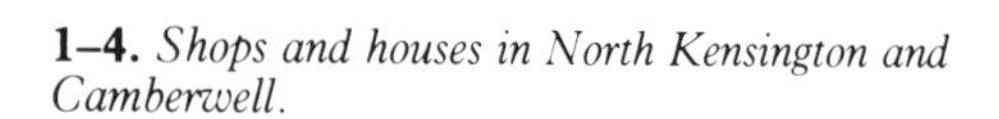
1–4. *Shops and houses in North Kensington and Camberwell.*

5–11. *'Street Art' has a respectable ancestry in the folk murals of southern Europe, and the much earlier murals associated with the Christian church, which have their origins in the early civilisations of the Mediterranean. It can be naive* **5**, *descriptive* **6**, *accidental* **7**, *nationalistic* **8**, *purely decorative* **9**, *combining decoration with commerce* **10**, *or architectural* **11**. *In most cases it evokes a special response from children, who should be allowed to participate. The architectural example is a trompe l'oeil painted upon the wall of a building in a blocked railway arch in bright colours. (Design by the author.)*

7

8

9

10

11

1

3

4

2

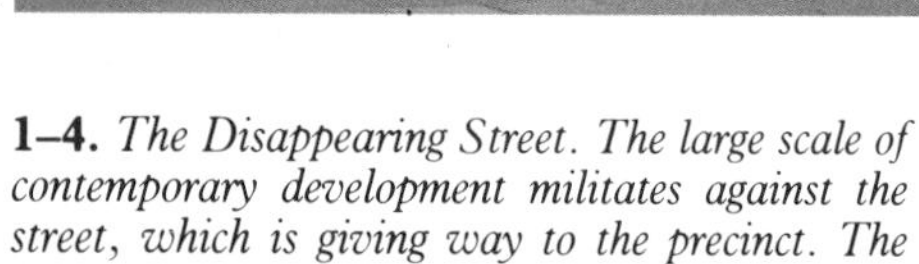

1–4. *The Disappearing Street. The large scale of contemporary development militates against the street, which is giving way to the precinct. The street is also visually disappearing due to the use of mirror glass. The technique has led to a surprising number of possibilities using different forms, different patterns, and different colours of mirror-glass. The architects of the shopping centre at Milton Keynes* **2** *chose to reflect the landscape, those at Tottenham Court Road to reflect the sky* **1**. *Norman Foster, in his dramatic understatement in Ipswich, the surrounding streets* **3, 4**. *But at night his building comes alive with colour.*

5–10. *Theatrical Architecture. Mirror is also used by Terry Farrell to give a distorted street image of TV AM. The sign has become an architectural symbol, the bright analagous colours of the architectural street façade run into a kind of stage through which the building is entered* **7–10**. *The most intense colours are used only as outlining elements, on narrow surfaces, like those at Warwick University Arts Centre which vary round the facets of the roof* **5, 6**. *(Architects Renton, Howard, Wood and Levine.)*

5

6

7

8

9

10

1

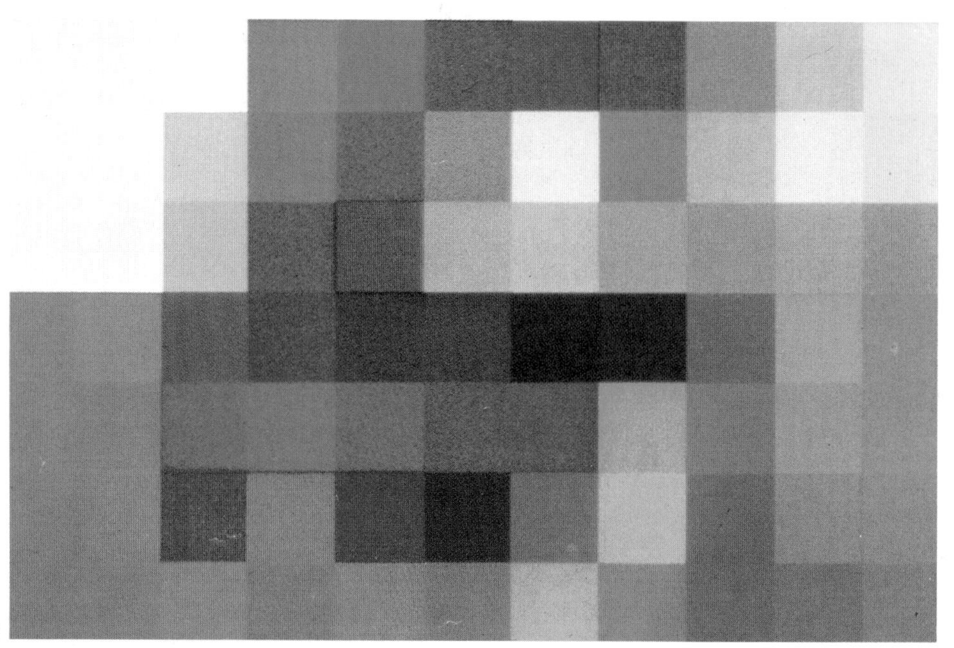
2

3

4

5

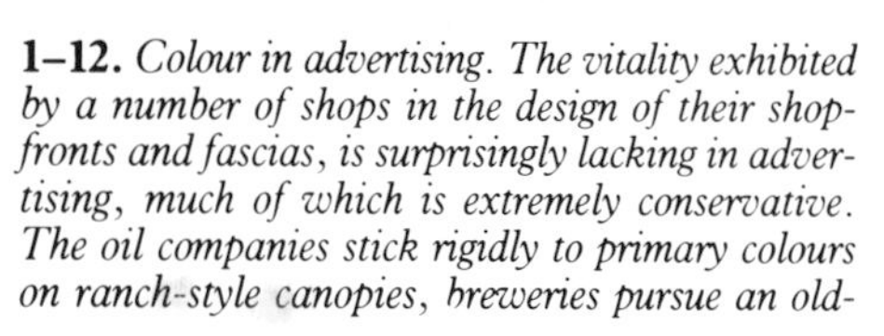

1–12. *Colour in advertising. The vitality exhibited by a number of shops in the design of their shopfronts and fascias, is surprisingly lacking in advertising, much of which is extremely conservative. The oil companies stick rigidly to primary colours on ranch-style canopies, breweries pursue an old-world charm and placard advertisers persistently fail to realise the enormous visual potential of their material. A rare exception is the witty fascia of a south London optician on which the shapes of spectacles are outlined in 'advancing' and 'receding' colours and set up a visual dialogue* **12**. *Also the advertisements of a cigarette company in which squares of pure hues of varying lightness and intensities are juxtaposed in what at a distance appears to be a picture; and close-to as an abstract composition of harmonious colours* **2, 6**. *(***4, 5, 8, 9** *by Stephen Lancaster.)*

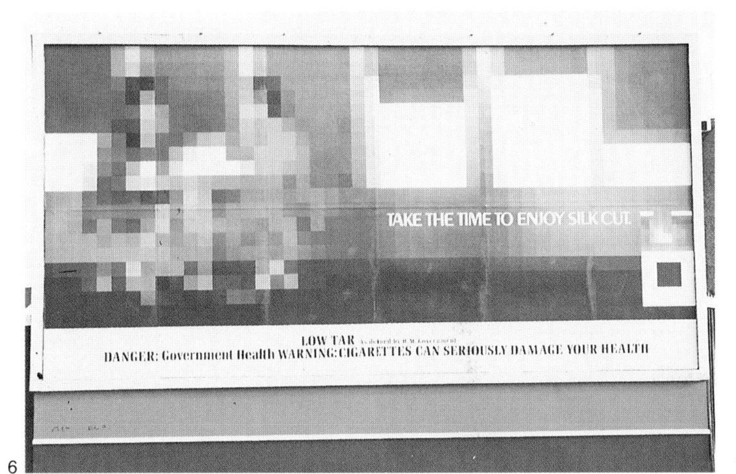
TAKE THE TIME TO ENJOY SILK CUT
LOW TAR
DANGER: Government Health WARNING: CIGARETTES CAN SERIOUSLY DAMAGE YOUR HEALTH

6

LIGHT COMMERCIAL VEHICLE SPECIALISTS
G. H. MOTORS LTD

7

8

Gulf
Red Lion Garage
used cars
RENAULT
RENAULT
The 1984
Motor Show
No

9

EVANS SUPPLY
STORES
PAINTS GARDENING HARDWARE

10

amalgam

11

Hugh Orr
Optician

12

Colour and new structures

Everything expresses colour, whether it is the incidental colour of a natural or processed material, or colour that is deliberately applied for a specific effect. No colour is seen in isolation: all colours within the field of view relate to each other; when a new colour is introduced that relationship is changed. In the past when natural materials, stone and brick, thatch and tile were in common use, integration caused little difficulty. Local traditions and usage could cope well enough, although they have had to cope with a surprisingly wide variety of scales and materials. Now that those traditions have largely disappeared and we are faced with increasingly strong pressures for development of all kinds, often using synthetic materials, the problem of integration is becoming acute.

Colour in the town is often used to add visual interest. In the country the objective is likely to be different. The countryside at its best has its own coherence: a unity of geology, topography, soils, vegetation and buildings, which has its own mysterious logic. New buildings, particularly when constructed of synthetic materials, can easily disrupt that coherence. Each case needs to be considered on its own merits. In the case of rural amenity and farm buildings integration is usually desirable: that implies careful co-ordination in terms of siting, scale, form, colour and detail of the building and its surroundings. But integration does not mean concealment or imitation. Traditional buildings in fact rarely 'melt into their background': some degree of contrast is normal. Moreover, traditional buildings themselves vary considerably. New buildings should take these differences into account, and where some degree of visual emphasis is appropriate, as for instance in the case of a tower silo, it may be given.

Concealment is usually inappropriate for buildings. Where it is desirable for certain structures it can be achieved by burying, earth-mounding or screening with trees and shrubs. This method can well be used to conceal the variety of untidy small-scale elements with which large industrial and power complexes are surrounded. Camouflage in the true sense of the word is something quite different, derived as it is from the French word *camouflét*, meaning smoke-puff. The idea of using abstract painting to conceal their battery had occurred to some artists serving in the French army in the First World War. It was developed in a 'Section de Camouflage', and later adopted by the British navy who applied zig-zag patterns of black, white and blue to disguise battleships. The Second World War provided many applications for different degrees of concealment and deception, of which the best known are the meandering patterns of brown, green and black. This is unfortunate because it tends to focus attention unnecessarily on the earth colours and distract from the many other interesting possibilities. It is in the striking distractive techniques of 'dazzle-painting' that camouflage has found an appropriate application today.[1]

Large industrial buildings cannot normally be concealed; rather we should have the self-confidence to express them appropriately. But a careful assessment of the site is necessary to decide exactly how that expression should be made. Where a number of new buildings are grouped together, as in industrial estates, they should clearly be considered together in terms of their form and colour, even if they are future projects. A colour policy needs to be established, especially if they are visible from a distance across the landscape. Large buildings may be changed, perhaps reduced in scale or altered in shape through careful use of colour, and parts of buildings may be given eye-catching emphasis. In every case a detailed study of site and conditions is necessary in order to decide clear objectives.

Some buildings frame the landscape. Foster Associates have gone further in designing the structure of the Renault Centre at Swindon like tree forms growing out of the landscape.

Colour and the farm

The farm provides one of the most cherished images of our landscape. It is a popular image, well sustained by countless publications, of peace, plenty and unchanging values. In reality farming is an industry, albeit our oldest, and like all industries it is subject to change. The evolution of the farm reflects the economic and social life of the country. While it is true that it can be of outstanding visual quality, a masterpiece created and sustained by landowners and farmers, it can also present a picture of chaos and even squalor. It is still possible, somewhat surprisingly, to look out upon a countryside which reflects in its field, patterns and buildings (and to some extent in its abandoned machinery and old cars), the values and technology of medieval, Georgian, Victorian and Edwardian societies, as well as those of today which are some cause for concern.[1]

The agricultural revolution which began in the 1940s has reversed the decline in agriculture which had persisted since the import of cheap wheat and chilled meat from America in the 1880s. The price we have had to pay is the loss of traditional labour and the mechanisation of our farms. A tractor is forty times more energy efficient than a horse. In addition the tractor has the capacity, thanks to a wide variety of attachments, to perform most of the operations that had formerly been undertaken by separate machines. The combine harvester, for one, can undertake, with a single operator, the work of a whole team of men which would formerly have been spread over a number of weeks. These changes have had a noticeable effect on the landscape: firstly there came a dramatic increase in the workable acreage, and secondly, there were changes in the buildings. Farms were amalgamated, fields enlarged and hedgerows uprooted. Also, stock production, first of poultry, then pigs and cattle, which had formerly been labour-intensive, moved out of the fields into industrial units. From a capability of supporting two or three urban families in the economy of the eighteenth century, the average farmer had with the steam power available in the 1870s, become able to feed some 35 people; now increased with oil and electric power, to about 100. In the interests of production such developments and the erection of new buildings were subsidised; supported by the Agriculture Act of 1947 which provided an economic base of guaranteed markets and assured prices. The use of subsidies also provides opportunities for control.[2]

These new machines and new methods demanded new buildings: buildings which were both large and flexible enough to accommodate the changes which were likely to occur within a ten-year period. Of course large buildings had existed before: all farms had barns, and some, such as the thirteenth-century tithe barn at Great Coxwell in Berkshire (measuring 46 metres long by 14 metres high), were extremely large. But the old traditional buildings had two disadvantages – they lacked flexibility and they needed maintenance, which in the absence of manpower was no longer available. The Dutch barn, now a familiar element of most farms, was introduced as long ago as the 1880s to solve such problems: namely, to combine maximum coverage with minimum obstruction and maintenance. Although far from being inconspicuous, the Dutch barn, by virtue of its simple functional shape, its honest expression of 'difference' from the traditional buildings, and its colour (originally red or black), could usually be integrated acceptably. More recent buildings however are remarkable for their number, scale, size, differing shapes and location. While traditional farms were often conceived as courtyards providing protection from the weather (and perhaps originally from attack), the modern farm, operating like a factory, tends to be linear – or even radial – in plan[3]. Siting in sympathy with existing buildings thus poses particular problems which need to be considered in careful conjunction with all the other factors involved. The problem is twofold: how to integrate the new, and what to do with the old. Fortunately, many organisations are expressing their concern by recording and sometimes conserving historic farm buildings. But the cost is high; and the threat of redundancy cannot be ignored: in 1972 it was estimated that in Suffolk, over 40 per cent of traditional farm buildings had not been used for ten years, and it was predicted that by the end of the century 90 per cent of farm buildings would be new. Our difficulty is to adapt to such dramatic change. Without accepting Wibberley's gloomy prediction that the countryside will in future be divided between the useful and the beautiful[4], we need to find ways in which the elements can be selected and integrated to form a new agricultural landscape as acceptable and as beautiful, although different, as the old.

New farm buildings

A cursory examination of traditional farm buildings throughout the country reveals a wide variety of design approaches expressed through siting and arrangement, building form

Berwickshire, Scotland. The farm and the landscape are indivisable. In this part of the country exposed to the cold east winds, farms lie along the river valleys. The one in the foreground is expanding and the new white shed has become a conspicuous visual target eclipsing the old buildings.

and detail, and colour given by materials and texture. A few built of stone, typically in rocky areas, appear to 'melt into the landscape', others to dominate it like fortresses. Many are small and informal, particularly in the uplands, compared with those in the low arable lands. Some of these built in the eighteenth and nineteenth centuries in East Anglia are inordinately large and dominate the flat landscape for miles. Materials generally have a local relationship – until late in the nineteenth century, having originated on the site. In their natural and applied colour there is a bias towards earth colours: reds, browns, ochres, greys and black and white. Weathering reduces contrasts by discoloration, and by the growth of lichens and algae, although slate is something of an exception. In general, in their relationship with the landscape, farm buildings are best seen in the middle distance, at which range the individual textures of tree-trunks and branches, leaves and flowers merge into uniform colours. At close range we focus on details and the landscape is excluded, and in the distance the buildings are lost. We read the landscape by picking out contrasts. Surfaces and colours of high reflectivity – such as white and yellow – and high chromatic content – such as red – will read strongly against a darker background[5]. Moreover, colours will contrast most strongly against those with which they have an opposite relationship, for example, red against green or blue. In bright sunshine the lightness will be accentuated by the contrast of shadows as well as the direct rays of the sun; by diffused light the surfaces of the building will appear to coalesce as a flat plane or planes according to their different textures and colours, silhouetted against the landscape background. The direction of the light is also important: colours are emphasised by the light coming from behind the observer, reduced when seen against the light. Thus we will read and identify a building by its form expressed in sunlight quite differently than from its unshadowed silhouette.

Recognition of the essential relationship between traditional farms and the landscape is necessary for the effective consideration of new buildings. To be properly integrated these should embody the same degree of contrast as the existing traditional buildings amongst which they are sited, or a contrast appropriate to their landscape setting. Concealment, even if effective, is inconsistent with our indiginous traditions. In fact it would be necessary to soften the form of the building as well as providing colours to suit seasonal changes effectively to hide a building. The best that can be done, and the most that is usually desirable, is some integration with the land form and judicious screening with trees; both traditional solutions. Ideally the new buildings should be accepted as functional necessities which can be treated sympathetically and seen as visual assets to the farm as a whole. To achieve this it is necessary to consider every detail, including siting and alignment, form, texture and colour.

If the building is placed close to other buildings, whether or not they are traditional, there will be a visual relationship between them, a *colour attachment*. The eye will pick up differences in scale, differences in roof pitch, differences in detail. Ideally roof pitches should match those existing. This is however rarely possible because traditional pitches tend to be much steeper than modern ones, due to the short spans and the materials used. In such cases the buildings should be orientated so that the differing roof pitches cannot be seen together. An exceptionally long roof-line may be broken, or swept down to a low level to match that of the existing buildings. The building may be cut into the slope to reduce its impact: on the other hand, if the building is isolated, it may – particularly if it is on the skyline – become a landmark. This is true of tower silos, which are difficult to integrate with other buildings. Viewed in the historical context of such features as windmills they may become acceptable landmarks.[6].

The materials first used for modern agricultural buildings – corrugated iron, concrete and asbestos-cement – were all basically light in colour, creating an unusually high degree of contrast in the landscape, particularly with regard to their roofs. Some of them also had the disadvantage of being resistant to weathering as well as the application of paint. More recently, materials and paints have been improved, but there still remains the problem of light-coloured walls and, more particularly, roofs. There is also the problem of shiny surfaces of dark buildings appearing light through reflection. Light buildings are more conspicuous than dark ones, and they seem larger. Moreover, the effect of size is exaggerated when the roof is also light in colour. The roofs of traditional buildings invariably look darker than the walls (except when seen against the light), even when they are of a similar colour. This is because the shadows of the tiles visually mix with their colour. It occurs less in the case of slate, but then it is counterbalanced by the relatively darker colour of the material. The general effect of this is twofold: it reduces the apparent scale, and it helps to 'anchor' the building to the ground[7]. Also, with natural materials there is often a visible or 'sensed' relationship, between land and building. There may however be occasions in which a desirable colour affinity might be established with exposed mineral surfaces, as for instance, between the 'whites' of asbestos cement and exposed chalk, limestone or china clay.

In general, within the limitations of blending with existing materials, darker colours should be chosen in preference to lighter: roofs should be textured and of a darker colour than the walls. Large light surfaces can also be broken down, in the way in which traditional buildings are subdivided, by the details of eaves, gables and modulations of wall surface. It may for instance be possible to punctuate the surface by picking out the structural elements and fascias in dark or other contrasting colours. The use of strong hues should also be confined to such relatively small areas, or to windows and doors, those traditional repositories of colour. The large surfaces of barn doors, however, read strongly in the landscape, and where a colour tradition exists, as is often the case, it should be respected. The importance of regional colours lies in the paintwork as well as in the natural materials.

When choosing colours, each situation must be considered on its own merits. Green, if not actually discordant, has an ambiguous relationship with the greens of vegetation. The reason is that the greens, like the other colours found in nature, are not simple: they are made up of large numbers of variations produced by light reflected from a multitude of different surfaces which are themselves individually coloured. The palette of nature is more subtle than that of man. It is thus pointless to expect a simple area of green paint, especially the intense apple, viridian and 'tart' greens much favoured by architects for industrial buildings, to do anything other than kill the vegetation colour. They should never be seen together. The more muted yellow-greens, khaki and a green so dark that it is almost black (called in France *wagon vert*), can however be used in the landscape, but with caution. Contrast is important. The persistent tendency to assume that things should be painted green to match nature is misguided. We should be guided rather by the browns, grey-browns, umbers and ochres of the natural landscape. Dark blue can sometimes be effective and always black, or, for an expressive element, white. But we should be aware of the pitfalls of using the bright, eye-catching colours of agricultural machinery, which are entirely appropriate for their purpose but not for permanent buildings in the landscape.

Silos of various kinds, which are an essentially new element in the landscape, have something of the dramatic possibilities of windmills, without their old-world charm. Rarely, however, can they be effectively integrated with traditional buildings. But if their essential tower form is acknowledged, a satisfactory relationship can usually be established. They should not normally be so dark in colour that ►

1. *The stone walls blend with earth and stubble, the roofs with the dark belts of trees, expressing a rare unity of colour. (Photograph Paul Walsh, Countryside Commission).*

2. *Fife, Scotland. Farm on a hill. The farmer likes a view of his land. This one has chosen a vantage point on top of a knoll and painted his house white to make sure everyone sees it.*

3, 4. *Derbyshire. The traditional white limestone walls and buildings of the Peak District can accommodate new white elements more easily than most. The new buildings, although somewhat untidy in disposition, are well-integrated by virtue of their black and white 'colours'.*

5. *Linear expansion. Modern farming methods often demand a linear arrangement of buildings in contrast to the courtyard planning which was common in the past. The development here appears to be piecemeal and the new light-coloured buildings have become unnecessarily conspicuous on the skyline. Fife, Scotland.*

6. *This white building on the edge of a field in Oxfordshire relates to the sky, making a 'hole' in the skyline. Had it been dark coloured or black it would have been lost against the background of trees.*

1

2

3

4

5

6

1

2

3

4

the form is lost against the background, nor so light that they become too conspicuous, unless they are seen against the sky, in which case a light colour may be desirable. A problem arises when they are seen against both sky and landscape, suggesting a colour that contrasts with both, with possibly a lighter roof colour. In certain cases they may be treated as bright focal points in the landscape by the use of strong colour[8].

In line with developments in materials and their finishes, a study has been made by the British Ministry of Agriculture and the French BAP, on the weathering and colouring of asbestos cement sheeting and its equivalents[9]. Although there are situations in which it may be considered desirable to use the natural colour of the sheeting either as a visual contrast or to blend with certain elements such as an exposed limestone outcrop, some form of colouring or darkening is generally preferred to make it less conspicuous in the landscape. Natural weathering and colonisation by lichens takes time and it can only occur satisfactorily where the air is reasonably pure; also it does tend to produce a mottled effect that is at odds with the precise nature of the material. On the other hand it is possible to colour the sheeting with suitable landscape colours.

The French study included experiments with a number of different chemical treaments of metallic salts, which give colours ranging from light beige through a range of greyish-yellows, orange-reds and browns through to ►

1. *In this view the similar shapes but diminishing sizes of the two white roofs relate well to the slope of the hillside, but less so to the buildings adjoining them. Their highly reflective quality makes them visible for some distance. Scotland.*

2. *Llanberis, North Wales. The grey blacks of the slate roofs blend with the slate mountain from which they came and the stone walls relate well to the vegetation. But the white shed roof has become the visual focus for the whole ensemble, distracting from all the other elements.*

3. *The small farm near Welshpool has expanded twice; once, including the red Dutch Barn which has a pleasing landscape relationship, and the second time adding two bright aluminium silos. Although attractive in themselves they relate poorly*

5

6

7

8

to the other buildings and provide a disconcertingly bright visual target in the landscape.

4. *Multiple buildings. These have obvious rhythms of their own, as seen in repetitive roofs of similar form and pitch, a character which is not difficult to achieve with modern buildings. In both these examples the materials are in characteristically subdued 'traditional' colours. But this Oxfordshire barn has acquired a new material, asbestos, which has weathered sufficiently to begin to blend with the slate.*

5. *Multiple buildings. Light grey limestone, grey slate, black weather-boarding. This much larger example near Preston in Berwickshire depends upon the large stone roof of the main barn and the long stone wall in front for unity, and upon sunlight and shadow to stress the rhythms and to differentiate between the surfaces of uniform material. The effect is spoilt by the white roof at the end.*

6. *Cotswold farm. Rhythm in two dimensions: of shapes, textures and material colours. The piece-meal roofs of stone, black corrugated iron and slate and the brown weather-boarding are to some extent unified by colour. All work in contrast of value with the yellowish limestone.*

7. *Snape, Suffolk. The colour composition is limited to the small barn on which the white door provides an irresistible target against black weather-boarding walls, distracting from the miscellany of other buildings. These are linked by their colour with the stubble and the lichens on the weathered asbestos roof of the barn. The East Anglian tradition of tarred weather-boarding and white paint departs here from the common tradition of darker roofs, working in this view as a two-dimensional colour composition reminiscent of Passmore at Peterlee.*

8. *Goathland, North Yorkshire moors. Originally farmers shared accommodation with their animals, each benefiting from the warmth of the other. This has given rise to a linear form which persists in the uplands of the north and west, with the house in the centre and the farm buildings arranged in descending order on either side, suggesting a geometrical progression. The white gate and windows contrasted against the dark brown gritstone clearly distinguish the house, and the red pantiled roof fixes it in the east.*

1

black, and one shade of pale blue. Their aim was to find a way of blending the colour of the sheeting, at the outset, with the other colours of the landscape, and more particularly with the coarse-textured Roman tiles common in the southern parts of France. As in British experiments, it was found that dilute solutions of ferrous, manganese and copper sulphate produced 'a patchy light brown' colour which darkens when it rains. In the French experiment the orange-reds produced by iron salts approximated to the rust colour on corrugated iron and other corroding iron surfaces, a common and acceptable landscape colour. The manganese produced similarly acceptable colours ranging from light yellow to dark brown.

Similar earth-related colours have been produced in wood stains and paint ranges. The former, which have long been used by the Scandianavian countries, have the advantage of adding a more or less strong translucent colour without hiding the attractive qualities of the wood grain. The British Standard Framework of Colours on which many paint ranges are based, has been developed from natural material colours occurring in the landscape, on the lines of the chromatic palettes developed by Lenclos. We now have wide ranges of material and methods at our disposal: our only difficulty is learning how to use them effectively.

Caravans

The caravan is by nature a clumsy vehicle. Lacking the functional neatness of either the narrow boat or the gypsy caravan, it is ungainly both in its mobility and its appearance. Its dual nature makes it appear at home neither on the road nor parked next to the house, whose role it seems to usurp. Tractors – like cranes – we can accept for their functional honesty of appearance. We accept cars also to some extent, but caravans disturb us by their ambiguity, so often do these seem out of their element, hybrids between houses and cars. Apart from their shape, their presence is emphasised by their predominantly light colour, as though they were insisting on their domestic rights. Two reasons are given for this: firstly that the colour is necessary for visibility on the road (although this is not demonstrated by the motor industry); secondly, that light roofs are necessary to reflect the heat, a factor for which it would be possible to compensate.

2

3

4

5

The problem is manifold. On the one hand it lies with the manufacturers; thereafter it rests with the users; on roads, by farms, in fields and on caravan sites. It rests also with the authorities. Permanent caravan sites clearly provide the best solution. Some of these are extremely well designed with proper access and services, and individual or group bays, as well as the perimeters, screened by trees and shrubs. Because caravans are not very high such screening can be easily achieved in lowland country. Concealment of this kind is more difficult in the uplands where sites can be viewed from above. It also costs money, and the pressures to fit as many caravans on site as possible – even if only during the summer, cannot always be resisted. This is particularly obvious in popular seaside areas where vast numbers of ►

1. *Farm near Snape, Suffolk. Bright red pantiles, red brick and white paint place this farmhouse clearly in the eastern lowlands. They distinguish it also from the neutral greys of its outbuildings which are visually relegated to the background.*

2. *Brockham, Surrey. The dramatic use of red to accentuate the details of doors and windows is an interesting departure from local tradition, but the red used here is too intense, too pink, too widespread and too scattered in small areas to harmonise with the other strong areas of colour in roof, walls and grass. As a result, all of their sublety is lost. (Photograph Paul Walsh, Countryside Commission)*

3. *Simple green surfaces can never match the complex greens of nature. The users of these blue-greens near Warwick have failed to see the predominance of yellow-greens and reds in vegetation and the value of contrast for buildings in the landscape.*

4, 5. *In some areas there is considerable precedent for the use of red in the landscape, including red paint on doors and windows. But the ochres and red browns traditionally used are in sympathy with both natural materials and the elements of the landscape as in the farm near Cockburnspath, Berwickshire* **5**. *The details of their colour should be subservient to the building as a whole, unlike the burning Post Office Red which has been used on the other farm* **4**. *(Photograph Paul Walsh, Countryside Commission)*

1

2

3

Tower Silos

1. *These may become significant landmarks as windmills were before them. Their scale and purity of form demands attention which may sometimes be reinforced by using conspicuous colours. These in Oxfordshire are dramatised in this view by their simplicity, particularly the rust-red roofs, in relation to the adjoining buildings. Their isolation, their location at the meeting of hedge lines, and the tenuous relationship with the small tower on the hill are also significant.*

2. *When closely associated with other buildings they are likely to be less effective. The different sizes of this pair of towers increases their interest. The dark blue colour of the cylinders is generally difficult to distinguish from a dark green commonly used, or black, except at close quarters. But the reflective quality of the shiny surface is of great significance, making the sides and tops of the towers appear much lighter. This is an important factor when considering the colour as seen against a landscape background.*

3. *The relationship between the dark towers and the dark stone and slate buildings near Bangor works well, being marred only by the intrusive white gable. North Wales.*

New Farm Buildings

4. *The designers of the extensions to Fincham Hall farm recognised the importance of respecting the existing building forms, roof angles, and colours. All the colours of the large new building: dark grey, white and red, echo the colours of the older building complex, and combine in a simple harmony. (Photograph, Paul Walsh, Countryside Commission)*

4

5

6

5, 6. *Siting, model. A system of using coloured models to simulate new buildings in the landscape has been developed by Prof. A. C. Hardy at Newcastle University in conjunction with the Council of Industrial Design. The colours are taken from the Munsell system. (Photograph and Method developed by Professor A. C. Hardy, Countryside Commission)*

7. *Colours have been used to unify where forms inevitably contrast in this large extension to an old Cornish farmstead. Most importantly, the roof colours are similar, but the colours of the lightweight wall cladding also relate well to those of the stone walls and winter vegetation in this view. Another important aspect is the way in which the scale of the new building is broken down by careful detailing, thus relating it to the scale of those existing. (Design and photograph, Richard Stratton)*

7

1, 2. *Dinas Dinlle, Snowdonia. The most conspicuous quality of caravans in the landscape is the way in which they reflect light* **1**. *This is largely due to the roofs, many of which are pure white. Greys, as seen in the examples in mid-Wales, are less obtrusive* **2**. *The sides come in many colours most of which in this group have a landscape affinity, with the glaring exception of the greenest green on the left which is hardly seen in nature.*

caravans of varied designs and colours congregate. The absence of any unifying screening elements easily results in visual chaos, the only alternative to which is some degree of control over the caravans themselves.

In a study undertaken for the National Caravan Council, Hardy investigated the role of colour in static caravans in relation to the landscape.[10] Having rejected the use of white and light colours of high reflectivity, he first considered the ideal of relating colours to the predominant colours of different regions of the country. But he rejected this as impractical, and instead, drew up a range of colours which would relate suitably to natural landscape colours in any part of the country. The aim was to be practical, consistent and limited, while maintaining sufficient flexibility for manufacturers to exercise commercial freedom. Hardy also considered the problem of thermal insulation as affected by colour. He found that the reduction of the Munsell reflectivity or lightness value from the present average of 6 to 5 (10.2%) could substantially increase the danger of heat bulging in the caravan body panelling – a factor which could of course be remedied in manufacture. In general, he was against the use of shiny and reflective materials, particularly on roofs, which are most easily seen from a distance, and in favour of colours with a maximum chroma (saturation) of 6 in the Munsell notation, drawn from a range weighted in favour of the 'natural' spectrum from yellow-red to green, and including a muted blue, but excluding purple and red-purple as inappropriate. Contrasting coloured panels were also considered undesirable because they attract attention. Like colour and shape, this is an important aspect of design which has to be considered when trying to achieve a balance between making the caravan look interesting both from the manufacturer's and the customers' viewpoint, and yet inconspicuous in the landscape. The range includes 22 colours, and it can be extended to include certain darker main body colours which still have acceptable heat absorbant qualities.

While the difficulties of any kind of national control are almost as insuperable as design control or motor cars, local control of permanent sites may well be possible, and it would be interesting to see some of the methods which have been applied to industrial buildings used creatively in this field.

Colour and industry

There is a relationship between character and activity which has its own special attraction. Like farms, industrial sites have their own particular kind of activity: who can resist the fascination of watching ships being unloaded, of building sites and, on a less public level, that of the extractive industries: mining, quarrying, sand and gravel extraction? This is not to deny the danger, discomfort and pollution – even squalor – of the industry itself. The fascination stems from a number of factors: the activity itself, our interest in machines and the recognition of a fundamental relationship with the materials and products of the earth. It has given rise in the course of time to a wide variety of tools, structures and buildings, some of which like the tin mines of Cornwall and the slate mines of Wales are now objects of archaeological interest. Some like gravel works, still have an antique appearance as they dig out the soft parts of the earth for us to see. Others, more modern, add brilliant splashes of yellow and orange to the disturbed landscape. Such local and transient uses of colour are usually, like the bright colours given to vehicles, acceptable and welcome for their association with particular activities. For one the essential functional tradition of the sea and ships, expressed in a unique visual language of black and white and coloured symbols, has been extended, via the canals, to the roads.

As industry becomes more complex, more automated and more segregated its traditions change. We are hiding its functions in megastructures, large flexible sheds of the kind that the farmer needs, which only occasionally exhibit their contents. These are developing a new aesthetic in their bold use of colour derived from such sources as industrial colour-coding, the motor industry and agricultural machinery, which adds an enjoyable new dimension to our experience.

Industrial buildings can be seen all around us: in towns, in the country, and increasingly in industrial areas or parks on the urban fringe. Some, like gas-holders, are seen in domestic surroundings, some against a background of green fields, and many new industrial buildings in close proximity with one another. Each must be considered on its own merits in relation to its location.

In general, the standard of design is high. The latest product of the functional tradition is a series of simple, factory-made sheds with clean lines and large unbroken surfaces. the whole subject of colour however is an area of unpredictability on which planning authorities are noticeably reticent. Norman Foster sums up the view of many architects in stating a liking for strong colours, 'an intuitive preference deriving from precedents such as the bold colours used on agricultural or contractors' machinery, or the eye-catching colours of advertisements.' Speaking on behalf os his own practice, he goes on to say: 'we enjoy the visual excitement of the juxtaposition of vivid colours and their effect on an object in the landscape.'[1] Such a policy leaves many questions unanswered. How, for instance, can the building be made to relate, in terms of colour, to its immediate neighbours and to its surroundings? How will it integrate with the landscape when seen from a distance?

The problem must be considered firstly in terms of location. For instance, where and from what distance will the building(s) be seen? At close quarters only the building and its near neighbours might be seen together, giving a limited palette of colours; but seen from a distance that palette could be widely extended, particularly in the case of an industrial estate on the edge of a city. The range of colours could be greatly expanded, creating difficulties of co-ordination for which only the planning authority should be responsible. Even when this is the case there is considerable margin for error. Planners cite numerous examples of shocked reaction to finished buildings which were approved on the basis of a minute colour swatch printed on paper or a verbal description of a colour. Co-ordinated colour policies are rare. Even the new town authorities, which might have provided good opportunities, have been tentative in this respect. Milton Keynes, where a basic principle of material colour zoning was adopted for housing, originally designated colour ranges for industrial areas. For various reasons, including the fading of some colours, these were changed on repainting. After administratve reorganisation, the individual area teams tended to develop their own colour policies, introducing more variety within areas. Generally there appears to be a reluctance to promote any overall colour-policy; the principle being to try 'to keep the options open', to persuade rather than to forbid and, constructively, to try to avoid too much contrast.

On the choice of colours, the basic principles apply. Dark colours will usually help a building to blend with the landscape and light colours will help it blend with the sky. For examples we may look to the precedent of dark weather-boarded farm buildings and light grey gas-holders. Dark colours, especially at the cooler

1

end of the spectrum, appear smaller than light ones. The analogy can be continued in terms of weight; colours being used to suggest also what is up and what is down[2]. The sense of gravity can be reinforced by the use of colours of graduated lightness and saturation from the base to the top or, for certain special effects, reversed. Such devices are being used to reduce or soften the impact of large blocks of flats in France, Germany, Japan and elsewhere.[3]

Large areas of bright colours should in general be avoided, because they are likely to dominate their surroundings, and may well create discordant effects in relation to other buildings. Also the eye soon tires, and the colour itself may well lose its appeal as well as its freshness during the life of the building. On the other hand, flashes of bright colour and small areas of brightly coloured detail can appear doubly stimulating against a relatively neutral background. This method might be used to stress the house colours of the manufacturer. The bright greens favoured by many architects should be avoided as colours which cannot attempt to match nature: grass – and even weeds – look pale beside them. Khaki and yellow-green, although appropriate colours, are usually too close to those of nature to provide the degree of contrast that the eye seeks, which is often found in farm buildings. But it is not necessary to be self-effacing. Colour may be used in many different ways to express the character and the spirit of the building, which can be austere or extrovert, according to the function and the intention of its designers. Colours can make it appear brighter or duller, larger or smaller, lighter or heavier, warmer or cooler: they can be used either simply or in combination. They can also be used to emphasise structure or outline, or to break down large surfaces by banding, whether horizontal, vertical, or diagonal. Alternatively they can be used in a more complex calligraphic way. More simply, adjoining sufaces can be differently coloured in order to 'de-materialise' form, thereby reducing bulk.►

1. *Occasionally, almost by accident, a dramatic structure arises in the landscape, like this stone quarry plant near Bampton. The simple variations of texture and colour in its battered corrugated-iron surfaces, give it an organic unity with the surroundings.*

2. *Gravel extraction plant, Thames Valley. Functional machinery, especially when seen in operation, has its own particular attraction.*

3, 5. *In Watney's brewery on the Thames at Mortlake, specific attempts were made to provide visual 'targets' using bright yellow for the tanks and silos. These become important river landmarks; they also have the function of distracting attention away from the large buildings at the end of the High Street, which have been painted light grey. The tanks and silos were originally intended to match, but the tanks are painted and the silos are cased in an industrially coloured plastic; on repainting the tanks became more intensely yellow.*

4. *Highly saturated hues, such as the bright yellow used at Watney's brewery, need to be restricted in area. Its dramatic dominance in the early industrial buildings at Milton Keynes overshadowed all else. But such excitement is difficult to sustain: the colour faded, and has had to be changed.*

2

3

4

5

1

2

3

4

5

But before any decisions are made, it is necessary to consider way in which the colours need to respond to a local or regional identity. Changes must also be taken into account, both in the surroundings in terms of light and seasonal changes of vegetation – including crops – and in terms of the expected life of the colour on the building. This will depend on a number of factors relating to the material, including the colour-fastness, the degree of cleaning required, and the likelihood of redecoration. Many brilliant designs have ultimately failed through neglect or excessive optimism.

1, 6. *Bright highly-saturated hues are best employed as 'targets' or framing elements. Yellow is used by architect Norman Foster to express the beauty of the structure in the new Renault Centre at Swindon. Happily, the Renault house colour is also a good landscape colour, here perhaps appropriately visible from a distance over undeveloped sites. The added dominance of colour to such a dominant structure will however not take kindly to competition.*

2. *Colour definition of form and structure has a respectable precedent in the tradition of half-timbered buildings. Although many were plastered or painted over, some, particularly in France and Germany, had their frames picked out in red or yellow. In this early industrial building, used for offices in Milton Keynes, the red (appearing pinkish due to reflected light) contrasts well with the white panels and green grass, but at the same time is not overpowering.*

3. *Red is also used effectively as a structural colour in Terry Farrell's new Thames Water Authority building at Swindon. But the columns here take on an almost ceremonial function, seen as they are against the 'recessive' blue. Red, like yellow, is a landscape colour. In this case the blue is muted by black, but brighter blues stand out in poor light, contrasting too strongly with the landscape greens.*

4. *Subdued or neutral coloured buildings can be enhanced by the addition of small areas of highly saturated hue, as in this industrial building at Swindon. The red and brown blend well with the yellow grasses, but such simplicity cannot long be maintained against competition from adjacent developments. (Architects Wyvern Partnership)*

5. *This green warehouse building by Farrell and Grimshaw is effectively enlivened by the red diagonal flashes but the green relates poorly to the grass. Gillingham, Kent.*

6

Colour and power

New farm buildings can be absorbed into the landscape, but where the largest structures are concerned there is no question of such integration. Buildings connected with energy or power, and occasionally defence, tend to be large and, unlike farm buildings, they have no direct traditional precedent. Each one, through an elaborate and laborious design process, has to be considered as a special case. They are the monuments of our civilisation, the castles and cathedrals of our time. Apart from the political, economic, social, ecological and technical problems, their design poses unique visual problems. Their large scale makes them conspicuous in the landscape, giving them an importance in the distant view and a dominance in the near and middle distance. Only occasionally is concealment prossible, as in the case of the underwater marine power station at Saint Malo in Brittany, and the Dinorwig pumped storage generator underground in the old slate quarry in north Wales. Both have been well integrated; at the same time providing an opportunity for the upgrading of the infrastructure of roads, services and amenities generally.

Partial concealment of oil tanks is common, for reasons of safety as well as appearance. These are often sunk into the ground, leaving the top few metres exposed, and relying upon siting and colour to reduce the visual impact. Siting is the result of a balance between quite complicated technological and aesthetic requirements; involving the layout pattern, the spacing between tanks, and their relative levels. Of all of these, it is probably the last which has the strongest impact when seen from a distance. A regular line of tanks seen against the skyline, is likely to be more obvious than an irregular profile. Once the siting has been satisfactorily achieved, the function of colour is to modify the effects of light in revealing the shapes of the tanks, either by total suppression or by some distractive means. The first has been employed at Flotta in the Orkneys[1], the second considerably earlier in the Amoco refinery at Milford Haven[2]. Both are in areas of high environmental quality. After a detailed colour study of the site and its vegetation from all significant viewpoints through all seasons the designers of Flotta drew up a range of eleven suitable colours which were then applied to photographs of various conditions of the site, in 66 samples. These were then evaluated by trained observers working on two groups, and reduced to one which was erected as a sample panel on site. A single colour, a dark reddish grey, was finally selected for the tanks; other colours, including some bright 'coded' colours, were chosen for items of detail. In the case of the Amoco refinery, where the tanks are collectively much more in evidence, the designers sought to increase spatial definition, firstly by using a variety of subdued colours and secondly by the use of a strong red to create a visual target. Both schemes offer interesting solutions: Flotta as a product of systematic and detailed colour analysis; the early Amoco refinery for the adventurous use of colour. While the latter suffers perhaps from too much variety, the severe restraint of Flotta which is emphasised by the level siting, calls for more. It is with some relief that we see the bright reds of the pipes in the close view.

Where it is possible to use form to express function, it is a valuable means of providing interest. It is a characteristic of such industrial elements as gas-holders and the cooling towers associated with power stations. The former have the added fascination of unseen movement, the latter are a product of a perfectly logical method of construction. The diabolo shape expresses both the function as a cooling tower and the structure formed by opposing sets of straight reinforcing rods held by ring beams at the top and bottom. It is a shape which also responds beautifully to changing light and passing cloud shadows. When carefully arranged in isolation these structures can enhance a landscape, but in areas of poor visibility their shape may coalesce with those of the other elements on the site, and seem undesirably bulky. This was the case at West Burton in the industrial atmosphere of the Trent Valley, where colour was introduced by the CEGB and their architects in 1961[3]. The aim was to provide visual differentation between the main buildings and the eight cooling towers arranged in a lozenge pattern. This was achieved by using contrasting cement colours in the cooling towers, two of them being picked out in dark grey and one in a dull yellow, against the 'standard' cement grey of the remaining five. The use of yellow on the cooling tower distinguished it as a point of reference seen from a considerable distance, even in poor light; com bined with the different greys of the other towers the spatial definition was highly successful. West Burton was the first power station in which colour had been used on a large scale, and it is unusual in that it has won awards from both the Civic Trust and the Countryside Commission.

Cooling towers disperse evaporation and

Amoco Oil Refinery, Milford Haven. (Architects Gordon Graham & Partners: architects and landscape consultants)

have industrial associations; the white spheres of Fylingdales conceal their purpose. The idea of siting an early warning station on the north Yorkshire moors inevitably invited public criticsm. In the event, the designers appear to have produced an ideal solution, combining functions of use and of structure with an ideal form and the purest 'colour', which actually enhances the site. It is true that the heavy concrete bases can be seen close-to – as can the facetting of the polyhedral domes – but from a distance the detail is lost: 'colour' and shape work perfectly, the white spheres floating over the dark moor make us oblivious of their ominous purpose.

Form should, in general, express function in buildings. In rural areas the landscape may also be a strong determinant of character. The building may have the territorial impact of a castle presiding over its domain, and its form may even hint at that. The main building of the nuclear power station at Trawsfynydd in north Wales is treated in such a way. Seen from the village it is fortress-like and uncompromising in the wild craggy landscape (a hundred years ago it might well have been disguised as a castle), and its colours – the grey of natural concrete combined with applied grey-brown panels – seem appropriate. Here much care has been taken, at some extra expense, to retain landscape features such as a small woodland, to site the untidy ancillery buildings and structures at a lower level out of sight, and to keep the rural character of the approach road by avoiding the common urban paraphernalia of street lighting and concrete kerbs. On flat and low-lying sites the building may also be allowed to dominate and given its own individual expression, as occurs at the two nuclear power station on the river Severn, at Oldbury and Berkeley, and at Sizewell on the Suffolk coast. These rely largely upon form reinforced by the limited use of colour for their effect. The problem however may not be so simple: for instance, proposals to build a second reactor in a different form of building alongside that at Sizewell are currently at public inquiry, and if approved may result in a third, thereby severely taxing the skills of the architects. Where such large structures are multiplied, colour will become increasingly important in the achievement of a balanced visual effect.

An attempt at colour integration has been ►

1

2

3

4

5

6

7

'Tank farms' have become a relatively common sight in various parts of the country. Some of the visual problems associated with their integration are illustrated here. At Flotta detailed colour studies carried out through the seasons indicated the use of a warm reddish grey as the best background colour **1**, *with the details picked out in bright colours including red. Partial concealment by burying the tanks is clearly an advantage, but the effect is prejudiced in this view by the level siting which causes their forms to coalesce when seen in diffused light; moreover the interest created by the bright colours does not register at a distance* **2**.

An alternative is to use one bright colour as a focus, against a background of more neutral colours, thereby increasing the depth of field, as has been done in the much earlier example at Milford Haven, **page 101**. *The eye is irrestistably drawn to the bright red, being distracted away from the tanks in the background. The other colours are however too varied, giving a sense of restlessness. This has been avoided in the smaller industrial plant at Le Havre, where the background colours are more closely related* **4**.
Flotta Marine Terminal, Orkney Islands. (W. J. Cairns and Partners, Environmental Consultants, Edinburgh. (Photographs, W. J. Cairns and Partners)

3, 6, 7. *Rust helps with the job of colouring gas-holders, producing interesting combinations. Very occasionally they are carefully painted in bands of analagous hue in ascending order of lightness; sometimes they are painted green in the misguided impression that they will be lost in the landscape. But usually they are painted a light greenish-grey which makes them remarkably inconspicuous in the town* **6**. *Gas-holder, Fulham, (cooling towers). The sculptural diabolo shapes of cooling towers derive from their function and mode of construction* **7**. *The normal colour is that of natural cement which is occasionally varied by using different coloured sands and cements. At West Burton one tower was coloured a dull yellow as a focus and two in dark grey to give increased spatial definition, avoiding the effect of coalescence when a large group is seen together from a distance in dull weather* **3**. *(Architect Rex Savidge, Photograph C.E.G.B.)*

5. *The white spheres of Fylingdales Early Warning Station appear disembodied symbols of the space-age, hovering over the North Yorkshire moors, constantly changing with the light.*

1

2

3

made at the nuclear power station at Wylfa on the north coast of Anglesey, where formal expression of the reactor has been combined with a careful use of colours appropriate to the region. Here exposure to a wide range of views from the surrounding high ground prompted the landscape architect to create a small range of wooded hills using surplus excavated soil; thus reducing the impact of the larger buildings and concealing some of the smaller ones and the cable towers. The success lies neither in concealment nor camouflage, but in the choice of colours applied to the cladding of the buildings. These include a greyish green, a pinkish brown, dark brown and black. The soft green relates well to the pale colours of sea and sky, particularly when it is subtly modulated by the different facets of the reactor tower; also surprisingly, it relates well to the strong greens of the grass and the slate walls. The light pinkish brown blends well with the exposed soil. From the low coastal plains where the scale, number and variety of the buildings is most apparent, the dark brown and black work simultaneously as unifying and distracting element, diverting attention from the smaller scale elements which can be so disturbing on this kind of site.

The distractive use of colour – that is using colour to create abstract images which can be visually separated from the object – harks back to Mondrian and the cubist experiments of Corbusier, and to an interesting example at Fawley oil refinery. The designers here avoided the problem of the cylindrical tanks, concentrating on giving interest to the large rectangular plant building in the background. This was achieved by the use of three different ►

4

1, 2. *In the distant view the power station at Trawsfynydd in Central Wales dominates the landscape like a fortress, and the greys and browns are appropriate colours* **1**. *But the arrangement of the lighter coloured panels with a strong horizontal emphasis, seen in the close view, detracts from the powerful image* **2**. *Some care has been taken, however, at considerable extra cost, to keep some of the ancillary buildings at a lower level out of sight, and to preserve the rural character by avoiding the usual paraphenalia of concrete kerbs and street lights on the approach road. (Architect Basil Spence and partners, Landscape Architect Sylvia Crowe)*

3, 4. *The power station at Wylfa on the north coast of Anglesey depends more upon colours to relate it to the sea and sky as well as the land. The muted grey-green of the main reactor building appears in a series of panels of different degrees of lightness on the facets of the reactor tower, which relate well to the changing colours of sea and sky. These colours, also relate surprisingly well to the greens of the slate walls and fields, as does the pinkish brown chosen for some of the cladding. The darker brown and black work well in breaking down the massive effect of the building complex, thus highlighting the effect of the other colours, and suppressing minor elements which would otherwise be visually disturbing. (Architects Farmer and Dark, Landscape Architect Sylvia Crowe)*

1

2

3

4

1, 3, 4. *At Littlebrook power station the idea of distractive colour has been developed further. Here it works in three dimensions. From a distance one is first aware of the black-topped grey chimney contrasted with horizontal panels of deep yellow ochre, a colour derived from that of local sand and gravel* **1**. *This successfully distracts from the old buildings, pylons and litter of materials around. As one moves closer the yellow panel is seen to be three-dimensional, part of a building working in a composition with white and what first appears to be black but becomes brown on closer inspection, divided by narrow bands of red, with the yellow above in the background* **3**. *Finally, the entrances are signified by green, the green doors being seen against a lower wall of concrete with exposed aggregate relating to the stones in the foreground, and an upper wall of white, beautifully marked by three small rings of red around the porthole windows* **4**. *The whole is a carefully orchestrated exercise in colour; the only false note is the use of the greens which make the plants look dull; in this case, the plants are in the wrong place. The beds of stones have a much better colour relationship with the concrete panels of the building. (Gordon Graham & Partners: architects and landscape consultants.)*

Photographs: **3** *Jonathon Watkins,* **4** *Dave Bower, Architectural Photography, 35 Castle Gate, Newark, Notts.*

2. *Colour can be very effective in reducing the effect of bulk, as seen in this example at Fawley on Southampton Water. The bright orange doors are the centres of attention in this Mondrian-like composition of greys, black and white. It succeeds in four ways: it is interesting in itself; it is pleasantly balanced; and it distracts from the tanks in the foreground. Moreover, the achromatic colours relate well to the changing colours of sky and land. But it is a very rare example. (Architects Farmer and Dark)*

The practice of Architect's Design Group formerly Gordon Graham & Partners has for many years specialised in the use of colour in industrial buildings, principally in connection with the power industries which have a strong impact upon the landscape. Their approach is to view each project on its own merits in relation to the landscape and natural light conditions prevailing on the site. Investigations include examination of the colours of the surface geology, soils, vegetation, and the preferred colours of local building traditions. Colour is used in a variety of ways, but in acknowledgement of the fact that concealment is usually ineffectual their inclination is generally

5

6

towards an expressive use of colour. At the large scale of the landscape this is employed to focus attention, thus distracting the attention away from the recessive colours of the background structures: at the detailed human scale it is used in the manner of industrial cable coding, with areas of danger and security in red, handrails in yellow, and pipework in suitably selected colours. In this way the impact of the large elements is reduced and that of the small elements, at a scale at which their colour is not overwhelming, increased. Buildings are often suppressed by the use of deep dark coloured roofs anchoring them to the ground in contrast to the larger vertical elements. In general, the colour palette is weighted towards the red end of the spectrum, with an occasional essay in blue acknowledging particular light conditions. They insist on the importance of colour being considered not after the basic design decisions have been taken, but as one of those basic decisions which must be respected from the beginning to the end of the development, including its working life.

Apart from power stations for the Central Electricity Generating Board, including Littlebrook, the practice has carried out a number of projects for the British Gas Corporation. These include a series of storage tanks and compressor stations. Tanks are studied through models and renderings of alternative patterns and colours to suit various local conditions of landscape, settlement and as far as possible, natural light.

5, 6. *The colour scheme for tanks designed to relate to three different foregrounds: rural, industrial and housing with graded vertical banding of red, purple, white and silver. Partington, Greater Manchester.*

greys arranged in rectangles with black and white, forming the background to a single bright colour, orange on the door. The effect was simultaneously to reduce scale, increase depth, and provide a focus of interest. At Littlebrook power station the idea has been developed further, into three dimensions. A new station, Littlebrook D, has been built alongside the previous one, situated in the unremarkable and neglected landscape of the Thames marshes, in an area littered with old buildings, stacked materials, and the inevitable forest of pylons. But so effective is the use of colour that all of these can at first be overlooked. This works on three levels: from a distance one is first aware of the black-topped concrete chimney working in counterpoint with horizontal panels in deep yellow ochre (a colour derived from the local sand and gravel). As one moves closer the yellow is seen to be part of a three-dimensional composition of black and white. Closer still, the black is seen as dark brown veined with lines of bright red, and the yellow moves into the background. Finally, as one approaches the buildings, the entrances are indicated by bright green pods which relate to green doors. These are seen against a background of white above, with red porthole windows and exposed-aggregate concrete below relating to paving and pebbles on the ground. The colour experience continues inside. The whole is a carefully orchestrated exercise in the use of controlled colour modulated to relate to and guide both the distant viewer and the user. It fails only in the use of green – unnecessary anyway, and a colour that makes the plants look dull. Perhaps plants should have no place here.

The expressive uses of colour are well illustrated by a number of storage tanks and compressor stations constructed for the British Gas Corporation in a variety of landscape settings. In each case, after a detailed study of local conditions – including samples of earth, vegetation and existing building colours – the architects[4] sought a particularly sympathetic colour expression. In a scheme under discussion they have to deal with a covered coal conveyor which meanders over the landscape. One of their several solutions to the problem is to colour it in variably graded stripes of yellow ochre, red and brown, changing to blue as it passes through a pinewood, in order to reduce the visual impact. This is a remarkably creative solution. Here there is an analogy with the patterns and colours of insects and reptiles, in which colours can be said to work on two levels: expressively in the close view, and contextually at long range. It is very far from the general inclination to 'paint it green'.

1

2

3

1. *The building mass of Pembroke Power Station is in this view effectively broken up by colour.*

2. *Wisbech, Cambridgeshire. The exhaust stacks of the compressors are visually reduced in bulk by means of light and dark grey banding arranged vertically in contrast to the horizontal lines of the building designed to echo the fen landscape. The upper layer is mid-blue which is neither dark enough to contrast strongly with the sky nor light enough to visually separate it from the ground colours.*

3. *The compressor buildings at Saint Fegus, between Fraserburgh and Peterhead have black stacks and light grey cabs, with detail picked out in white, echoing the functional tradition. The dominance of water on the coastal plain on which the station is sited, suggested the unusual blue colour for the control building.*
*(***1–3** *Architect's Design Group)*

Colour and transport

Land transport systems serve both to unite and to divide. The canals, built largely in the fifty years following the opening of the Salford canal in 1761, are seen now as nostalgic backwaters, reminders of our industrial past. Once they were seen as miracles of engineering, carrying water over hill and valley with the imperious confidence of the Roman roads. Undoubtedly they were also seen, in an age when 'the picturesque' was becoming fashionable, as unsympathetic blots upon the landscape. Nevertheless, their divisiveness was small-scale, and balanced by a unity and simple honesty of design in small buildings, bridges, locks and their details, which we have recently come to celebrate as supreme examples of 'the functional tradition'. In addition, the nomadic communities of the narrow boats developed a new vernacular tradition of decoration. Their restrained use of red, green and yellow on their utensils and boats has a heraldic effect against the black and white of the background colours. This tradition links up with the folk painting traditions once seen on gypsy caravans, seagoing boats, and undoubtedly also on some buildings.

The railway companies created their own vernacular. Drawing upon the traditions of coachbuilding, they created their own livery and heraldic insignia. They gave different colours to the regions, which survived until nationalisation. Their spread was infinitely more extensive – and much more intrusive – than that of the canals, needing more land to be moulded into cuttings and embankments. However, because they were to a large extent the instrument of development and distribution of materials, rather than just the product, there are still considerable regional differences in the use of materials. They also provided opportunities for individuality in the colour schemes for stations; a kind of expression which survives in some small measure in station gardens. Central organisation does not necessarily mean uniformity, and a detailed study of ways in which the identity of geographical regions could be reinforced by the use of colour might provide interesting insights, and satisfying results.

Roads have their own special problems. The increase of motor traffic (and the economy that supports it) gives them a voracious appetite for land. They can thus, as in the case of motorways, be infinitely more obtrusive than railways. Unlike the railways, which were largely created at a time of regional separation using natural materials from which some degree of regional identity is derived, the motorways (and to a lesser extent the trunk roads) are a product of national resources: they are planned on a national scale, using nationally available materials – particularly concrete – and subject to standard specifications. All these factors militate against regional identity, yet so complex is the nature of the British landscape that in most areas a substantial visual contrast in topography, vegetation and traditional buildings, occurs every 10 miles, and in the flatter areas (such as East Anglia) every 30 miles. These changes are equivalent to between 10 and 30 minutes' travelling time.[1]

Colour in relation to roads must be considered from two points of view: firstly, that of the driver and passengers; and secondly, that of the observer, or pedestrian. Naturally there may be conflict of interests between these points of view. In the case of fast roads, such as motorways and trunk roads, where safety is all-important, colour has first to be considered from the point of view of its effect upon the driver, in terms of day and night vision with regard to such factors of glare and concentration. In general it is felt that road surface should have a higher reflective value than their surroundings to facilitate fast driving – a view perhaps not shared by the observer concerned about the effect of the road in the landscape. This is particularly apparent when the road is seen from high ground[2].

Examination of road surface colours, even those of motorways, throughout the country reveals a wide variety of colour finishes, all notionally conforming to similar standards of safety and durability. These colours are determined by the finishing materials: concrete or tarmacadam; and by the aggregate chippings. The latter vary from dark red through pink, brown, green, light and dark grey, according to their geological origin. Since all roads, particularly motorways, are subject to continuous wear and tear, surfaces are constantly being renewed, invariably without much regard for the colour of the adjoining stretches of road. It is thus possible in some areas to travel over a variety of different colour surfaces, because the choice of aggregate colour is often left to the contractor, provided he conforms to the appropriate engineering design specification. Where aggregates are specified by type and colour by county road authorities they are usually identified with surface types such as carriageways, lay-bys, footways and so on, rather than with specific types of roads or roads of regional character. (Bus lanes are being identified in many

1

2

3

4

1, 2. *Motorway bridges read as targets against the background. When built in concrete they are usually left unpainted, but steel elements such as joists and railings need painting for protection, and colour choices have to be made. In general the objective should be to provide a focus of interest which is not distracting, using a colour which unites rather than divides the two sides of the road. The olive-green succeeds in this where pale blue visually separates the abutments by relating more to the sky. The unavoidable distractive effects of the white lorries are also very noticeable.*

3, 4. *The sign has become an important target in this view* **3**. *To the driver the colour of bridge railings is significant, seen from a distance when the light-spreading colouring of the railings is dominant. As he approaches they become increasingly more evident until the gaps dominate the colour of the railings themselves. It is noticeable that red railings relate well to the landscape, and that blue can sometimes suggest the blue haze of distance* **4**.

5, 6. *Colour functions as an important element of direction: in the contrasted bands of woodland, green verge, pink berm and crops. Wild flowers are now also effectively spreading along 'botanical corridors' similar to those of railway cuttings.*

7. *Signs are often best seen against a background of vegetation, particularly when they are red, which is complementary to green. But there are too many signs and the background is messy.*

8. *On country roads white lines and kerbs should be kept to the essential minimum, to avoid a strong interruption in the flow of the landscape, which is reinforced by the presence of mature trees.*

cities in a similar way). In the same manner, the Birmingham city engineer differentiated between the inner, middle and outer ring roads by using red, green and grey-black aggregates[3]; and more recently the Milton Keynes authorities used a variety of coloured tarmacs for secondary roads in housing areas. Now that coloured aggregates are being used in the concrete of some motorway bridge abutments to give them a local character, we might consider reinforcing regional expression of colour co-ordination of the surfaces using local materials. Regarding the actual road surface, applied finishes such as white and yellow lines and reflective road-studs should be considered; for instance, the reflective colour qualities of white lines versus concrete kerbs on rural roads. Although most of these are imposed by regu-

5

6

7

8

lation, their colour signficance should not be ignored.

Road and motorway bridges pose a special problem. Unlike city river bridges which have special territorial and historic significance, the design of these is predominantly functional, and intended to be physically unobtrusive. The question of visual obtrusiveness is a difficult one since there is no doubt that most bridges to some extent express the idiosyncrasies of their designers. Two basic materials are used: steel and reinforced concrete. In general, the steel ones are painted for protection, but concrete can be left unpainted, unless, as is happening with some of the older bridges, repairs to cracked surfaces necessitate redecoration[4]. The colours chosen for this are neutral, expressing current policy in Britain which is generally against the use of strong colour. In Japan, however, and some continental countries bright colours are deliberately used. At a distance the bridge itself seems to be a 'target',[5] effectively closing the view which appears with increasing rapidity as the driver approaches. If its colour is highly reflective the contrast between the bridge and its surroundings is stronger and more distracting. If it is given a strong colour the eye is also distracted, especially if the colour only covers a part of the bridge, such as the spanning beam. The use of a shiny material or even gloss paint – compounds the problem of distraction. The grouping of steel bridges provides an opportunity for organised colour sequences: here the use of the more subtle coloured paints is less distracting, and can provide a welcome variety. A subtler approach for bridges with railings is for the railings to be brightly painted, as has been done on the M4. Here the railings first appear as a strong 'mist' of colour, which gradually diminishes as the gaps between the railings become more evident, until it virtually disappears like the massed colour of willow stems in the close view. In this instance the blue resembles the blue haze of distance; and the red may relate to the warm colours of the adjoining landscape. This would appear to solve the problem of contrast and distraction by a particularly simple, subtle visual device. Where this is not possible the use of a carefully selected range of muted colours could do much to reduce the effective contrast and to relieve the monotony of travel, giving a specific identity particularly in anonymous built-up areas. This can also to some extent be

1. *The bright 'pop' colours are an asset to this motorway service area at Hilton Park on the M6, but the green makes the grass look tawdry.*

2. *The opportunity to design buildings which adequately express the idea of fast travel is rarely exploited, as in the example at Corley Service Area, on the M6.*

achieved by the use of local materials for facing on the abutments, but great care has to be taken to avoid an attempt at imitation. The integrity of the bridge as an essentially modern kind of structure should not be impaired by any fake rusticity or classicism.

Bridges which vary considerably in their design due to the demands of different locations and engineering considerations, provide a good opportunity for some regional expression. Other artefacts, such as barriers and signs have functions which are inevitably more standardised. Barriers need to be functionally effective, visually discreet and easy to maintain. A natural galvanised finish (as applied to electricity pylons) used on small-scale elements, blends well with both road and landscape backgrounds.

Buildings also can be used to reinforce regional character, particularly when they are of small scale. By the careful use of colour and materials others through their imagery may seek to express the idea of fast travel, but this is a rare occurrence. Regional identity is a product much more of the landscape than the buildings. By careful planning and integration the road can be used to enhance that identity.

Colour and signs

Signs have their origin in pre-literate society. Shopkeepers used to hang objects or symbols of their trade above their shops until it was forbidden by law in 1762 because so many people were injured by falling signs. The practice continues in a small way with pawnbrokers, barbers, public houses and a few others. The pawnbrokers balls derive from three gold discs based upon Byzantine coins. The barber's pole was originally red with a bleeding dish at the end signifying the barber's role as surgeon. The patient would grasp the pole while being bled; a white bandage twisted round the pole gave rise to the spiral stripes[1]. In our multi-lingual society dependent upon rapid communication we are returning to the use of signs and symbols.
mation clearly and concisely. For this reason it must be a visual target, to a greater or lesser extent according to its importance. Motorway signs, clearly, must be highly efficient both in terms of visibility and imparting information. The factors which need careful consideration are: size and scale in relation to the surroundings, shape, colour, symbol or wording, siting and number of repetitions, as well as durability and fixing.

Shape is of particular importance in relation both to background and content. Rectangular signs are generally best for lettering and for mounting on walls, whereas circular ones are usually better for symbols and, being more perfect in shape, they are less obtrusive in the landscape[2]. The adoption of the latter with a red warning edge on white with black for mandatory road signs is appropriate[3]. But the use of colour in general leaves much to be desired.

In Britain we have a long tradition of signs and signwriting which has given us some outstanding examples, particularly in street names, shop fascias and commercial signs. The variety of lettering is extremely rich and something to be cherished and fostered. The city of Bath, for example, has a policy of incising street names in the stone of buildings at a high level where they can be seen, allowing for many variations on the basic form of English lettering. Hampstead uses white lettering on black ceramic tiles. Such local traditions, although costly, help to preserve the character of a place. Mass-produced lettering on the other hand can be an important unifying element. For example the sans-serif type designed for London Transport has become a model for many transport systems.

Black and white are the most legible, white being the most reflective, and therefore eye-catching, 'colour'. This is why white lettering on a black background looks larger than black on white, and if the spacing is inadequate the white letters may appear to merge with one another. Yellow is also highly reflective and is in general, like black, white and grey, a colour which fits well into the countryside. Strangely, it is relatively little used for permanent signs, except on vehicles. Red also works well in its complementary role to green, and is a universal symbol of danger. This somewhat precludes its use for information signs (although our reading of warning signs is frequently confused by a variety of other reds connected with petrol stations and shop fronts). The more natural red-browns and Venetian reds, as used for some rural direction signs in Denmark[4], would be a welcome addition. But it should be noted that red does not read by sodium light. Blue has an arresting but somewhat ambivalent character in the landscape. The light blue of motorway signs which 'chalks' with age, is currently being replaced by a darker, more purple blue; more easily visible, particularly during the day. Green, while acceptable in urban areas, should be avoided in the countryside. The use of dark green with white and yellow lettering on trunk roads tends to create a visual ambiguity with the background of vegetation, although the yellow lettering is very effective. The new, harsher green with which it is currently being replaced is much worse. Similarly, the standard Ministry of Works signs for ancient monuments in green and cream are unsuitable against a green background, apart from their rather tired period flavour. The use of green for rural signs, as for fencing and buildings, is misguided, expressing as it does a naive view of the countryside that is encapsulated, albeit in extreme form, in the pseudo-rusticity of waney-edged signboards and bus shelters.

With signs, as with everything else, it is necessary to consider the whole picture. Signs tend to multiply: once one has been erected, others tend to follow. While the shape and colour of one may be acceptable in a particular place, these qualities may conflict with others. Also, a type which is suitable for one location may be unsuitable for another. Colours best suited to the greys and browns of the urban environment may well not be suited to the greens of the countryside; an appropriate scale for a town is unlikely to be a scale appropriate for a village. Everything, from the location to the size, shape and colour, needs to be taken into account. This has been done for transport systems: some, like those for the canals and the

1

2

3

4

railways, date back for more than a century. It is now being done for the closed systems in airports and air terminals. But in the world outside chaos reigns. Everywhere there is a need for proper co-ordination of signs at the pedestrian level: in this colour, and colour coding, could play a most important part.

1. *The symbol. The white circle forms the perfect background for the sign of the Black Swan at Helmsley in Yorkshire.*

2. *Caernarvon. Here the message is less for the eyes than for the body as it passes through this hallowed doorway.*

3, 4. *Signs shaped to fit. The first has small lettering for local street consumption; the pub sign has to be readable across the river Thames.*

5. *Cerrigidrydion. The shape of the boards is so informative that the drawn arrow is scarcely necessary.*

6. *Trunk road sign. The reflective elements: the white rim, arrow, lettering and posts first catch the*

5

6

7

8

eye; then the yellow, then the green which although not a strong colour looks black against a much lighter background.

7. *The low height is appropriate, the green just dark enough for these signs in Kew Gardens. But the white lettering, like that on the blue sign, is as thick as it could be without 'spreading' into illegibility.*

8. *Black and white are appropriate 'colours' for the landscape, particularly of Wales. The composite nature of the board is useful.*

9. *Holyhead. Blue is clearly visible against green, and it hints appropriately at the watery nature of the nature reserve.*

10. *This simple piece of etched plywood is a suitable colour for a rambler's sign which should not be too conspicuous.*

9

10

Colour and materials

The colour appearance of any material depends upon the direction and composition of the light, the molecular structure and pigmentation of the material, and the distance from which it is seen. Further variables also arise from the area of the material in relation to the colours of adjoining materials, and of course the responses of the observer himself. We may note here the phenomenom of *colour constancy* by which the brain registers the known local colour of the material seen regardless of the illumination of the surface at the time. This can occur only when there is foreknowledge of the particular colour. Strictly speaking the local colour of the material can only be known in certain controlled laboratory conditions: in practice it is customary to make rather general assumptions. In rare cases a sample panel of the coloured material may be viewed on site throughout a whole year but this is rarely practicable; commonly it is for a few weeks or months. Often it is not at all, and the colour is selected from a colour swatch or a piece of material.

Distance reduces the sharpness of form and the distinction of texture, but it affects colour in a peculiar way: the colour becomes disembodied. When we move so far away from a brick wall that we can no longer distinguish the joints, their colour will have mixed with that of the bricks, presenting a simple panel of colour. As the distance increases, the colour becomes more divorced from the material, until when we are no longer able to distinguish the building, the colour remains an amorphous area.

Colour is never seen in isolation. The colour of the door furniture is seen in relation to that of the door, the door to its frame and the walls and windows, the walls to the roof and details of gutters and downpipes, the building to related buildings, and all to the (landscape) background. In our preoccupation to make all the other colours match up, the landscape background, or indeed foreground, is often forgotten. This is due in large part to its complexity, but also to its changeability. But without a proper consideration of its qualities successful integration is impossible. The texture and colours of plants are never simple. They arise from a wide variety of different surfaces, each of which is in a constant state of change due to movement, growth and changing light. The surfaces of building materials are by comparison, simple.

The texture of the material is important in determining the way in which the light is reflected. Thus it may be corrugated or even, rough or smooth, (or according to the finer distinction applied to paints, matt or gloss). In breaking up the light and producing shadows, a corrugated surface may be compared to waves in the sea. Light is reflected differently from the different surfaces, some appearing lighter and some appearing darker, according to orientation. If, although corrugated, the surface is smooth, some of the light will be reflected off as white light. Whatever the case, the overall colour effect of a corrugated surface will be darker than that of a similiarly coloured smooth surface. If, on the other hand, a surface is shiny, although dark in hue, reflection of light may make it appear lighter than a duller but lighter equivalent. This effect is commonly seen in tower silos, which are often finished with a shiny dark blue or dark green paint. In fact the shine is often rather more important than the colour. Moisture also makes surfaces shiny, as frequently seen in wet paving. It also has the effect of intensifying the hue so effectively, that this is sometimes done artificially by the application of lacquer. It is worth remembering that in the wetter northern and western areas of the country hues of materials are frequently intensified by a film of moisture. This also applies to the vegetation.

Pigmentation may occur in natural material. it may be applied in mixing or manufacture, or it may be applied as a surface colour. The much-celebrated beauty of natural materials is in their great variety and their unique individual textures and colours. Pigment can never be applied to such a degree of complexity. In bricks we can depend upon the effects of firing to create interest: but with concrete, asbestos and other manufactured products we have to rely upon other factors. Added pigments produce uniform colours, which when properly used can be very effective. But when they are used to simulate another material they are usually unsuccessful. An exception is compressed asbestos 'slate' roofing. These regular black 'slates' make a perfectly acceptable roof which may easily be mistaken for natural slate. The material also lends itself to the integration of other strongly saturated hues. Concrete tiles and bricks accept pigment less readily and tend to look either dull or too bright.

In general the subtlety and complexity of pigmentation decreases through the range of materials from the natural, through the processed and those with mixed or integrated colour, to applied colour. At the same time the intensity increases. Thus it is possible in paint or plastics to achieve a brilliance that will make

1

all other coloured materials look dull. Some, such as 'day-glo' paint colours, which have their place on the backs of lorries, may well be too bright for any building. Moreover the most intense colours tend to suffer from fading. All must be carefully considered in terms of an

1. *White, red and grey. The first two are seen from a distance as disembodied 'colours', the white being highly reflective, and the red being intensely saturated. The grey melts into the background. As we advance we can see their 'attachment' to roofs; but only when we get close can we see that the first is lime slurry, the second rusty corrugated iron, and the third slate. Snowdonia.*

2. *White on white. A composition of painted wood, painted render, and glass contrasted with warm brick and tile to which the render relates, and cool blue paint with which the glass is more readily associated.*

3. *Cream on cream. The colours of shadow, painted stucco, painted stone, Portland Stone, granite and York Stone, unified by the yellowish rays of the morning sun. Carlton House, Waterloo Place, London.*

2

3

1

2

3

4

5

6

area/intensity ratio: the more subdued, the larger the area they may be used to cover in relation to the whole.

Since area is a critical factor in the use of colour, materials can be usefully grouped into three categories: those giving background colour, those giving major surface colour, and those contributing to detail colour. The first comprises the landscape or building background, perhaps including roads and areas of paving. The second category includes materials for walls, roofs, large areas of glass, and paving. The third includes those that define structure and outline, and express doors, windows and other details. In this there is a long traditional precedent of colour being used to accentuate form and define detail.

Building in the twentieth century is marked by a search for new materials to cover large structures economically. Asbestos products, metals, glass and plastics, all have their place, as well as concrete, if their essential characteristics are respected. But for these, unlike traditional materials precision is all important. They do not respond well to cracks or chips, nor generally to the discoloration caused by weathering. Natural materials, on the other hand, age elegantly.

1. *The corrugated effect of old Roman tiles in Spain.*

2, 3. *Asbestos cement (and its more recent substitutes) is a material which looks its best when new: that is bright, sharp-edged and ridged by strong shadow lines. Weathering has the effect of turning it grey, or covering it with lichens and mosses. Although this has the advantage of making it inconspicuous at a distance, it does not age elegantly. Initial colouring is preferable.*

4. *White and whiter. The house on the left is rendered with a white mix containing white mineral chippings, that on the right painted with Snowcem. Berwickshire. (Photograph; Tom Turner)*

5. *Black and white tradition. Eye-catching white 'spreads' against the black painted background, which looks greenish. Workshop, Sussex.*

6. *The unifying quality of white. The bright contrast of this fence near Pershore leaves no doubt about the route or the boundary. Here, as in race courses, white is used positively. Used indiscriminately in the landscape it can be distracting.*

7

8

9

10

Fences and railings

7–11. *The colour of fences and railings needs especially careful attention, for it depends as much upon the detail as upon the applied colour. The rounded cruciform cross-sections of these railings at Barnes reflect light and colour in a wide variety of ways, the black, for example, sometimes appearing light grey when seen against the light. Of the colours which they are painted: green, blue-green, yellow-green and black, black is probably the best because of the constrast with the vegetation colour. The yellow-green is the best of the greens, having a close relationship with the natural greens, but all greens tend to have an ambiguous relationship with vegetation and they should be avoided. This applies particularly in the case of green plastic-coated chain-link fencing. The white gate in Wales is in striking contrast. (Photographs* **7–10** *Stephen Lancaster.)*

11

1

2

3

4

5

6

7

1. *Paving contrast. A web of white limestone setts at Raglan Castle reflects light in contrast with the dark joints. The organic quality is due to the subtle variations in size.*

2. *Yellowish-white limestone contrasts with brown York Stone. York.*

3. *New patterns, traditional materials. The pattern combines an intriguing series of geometrical progressions with the basic functional needs deriving form the alignment of the street and its drainage. Marburg, Germany.*

4. *Old patterns, new materials. The simple logic of this contrasting concrete paving based upon the ancient Greek key pattern, is refreshing. Rotterdam.*

5. *Simulated contrast. This traditional method of simulating moulded quoins with colour, creating an illusion, is still common in Ireland. London.*

6. *Contrasting colour effects can be obtained by using different coloured aggregates in pebble-dash. Scotland.*

7. *The effects of light can be very variable especially on corrugated surfaces like this at Gillingham.*

8. *Contrast of extension. Highly-saturated strong colours need to cover only small areas to register effectively in this way. Significant objects, such as post and telephone boxes, hydrants and signs, as well as bollards, become focal points in the environment. Red bollard on grey quay with white swans, Berwick. (Photograph, Tom Turner)*

9, 10. *Uniformity and dullness of hue are a characteristic of coloured concrete paving. More contrast in their use would be an advantage.*

11, 12. *Although effective and well balanced colours the brown and grey are eclipsed by the awkward pattern of the white. (Photographs, Stephen Lancaster)*

8

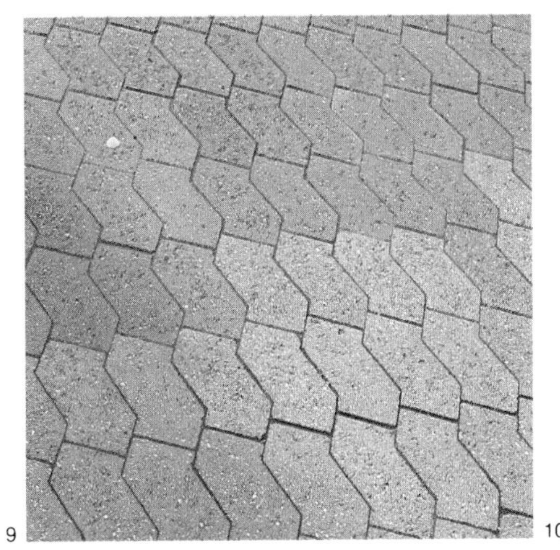

9

10

11

12

Colour guidelines

The complexity of our environment and the pressures for development of many different kinds emphasise the importance of colour and the way it is used. Although intuitive use should be accepted in a limited context, in the wider field it can easily be lead to visual chaos. As more and more mass-produced materials and buildings appear, like motor cars in ever brighter colours, we are in danger not only of squandering the remains of our beautiful towns and countryside, but of over-stimulating ourselves into a state of visual boredom.

In order to deal effectively with the problem it is necessary, firstly, to understand the nature of colour and how it is perceived; secondly, to devise methods of analysing the colour background against which any new development will be seen; and thirdly, to provide means of selecting and using colours appropriate to that background. Although the study relates primarily to this country, the principles can be applied to any context. They can be applied also at any scale, from the micro-scale of the front door and the sign-board to the macro-scale of the industrial complex or the power station.

The guidelines deal with colour. It must not however be forgotten that colour is only one of several aspects, including siting, form and detail as well as the physical effects upon the surroundings, which express the presence of a new structure. It is however, a most significant factor.

A colour decision is made every time a new object is introduced into the environment. In practice the weight given to that decision depends very much upon the size and nature of the project and the time and money spent on it. When politically sensitive items such as oil terminals and power stations are sited in areas of outstanding natural beauty time and resources may allow for proper consideration. But more often than not colour decisions relating to large and small industrial and commercial buildings are made on the basis of intuition or personal preference on the part of the designer or client, and communicated to the controlling planning authority by means of a perspective drawing rendered on paper, a small patch on a colour card, or at worst a verbal description. In the case of many farm buildings no approval is required. There are also innumerable cases in which it would be undesirable, even if it were practicable, to impose regulations. These are the idiosyncratic decisions made by individuals and small groups in relation to the personal environment: houses, front doors, windows, gates, fences; which collectively may give interesting variety. For colour is one of the great indulgences of our time. Planning authorities are properly concerned with maintaining a visually coherent environment. But the subject of colour is so elusive that it eludes even a majority of designers. Guidelines are necessary to assist in understanding the ways in which it works in the environment so that it can be used more positively, to greater creative effect.

The guidelines are intended for planning authorities and applicants for planning permission. They are set out in the form of explanatory notes and a questionnaire which can be used as a check-list, which should be of particular use in dealing with large and complex developments.

The guidelines are set out as series of sections describing the principal factors to be taken into account in making colour assessments and determining colour policies. In dealing with such a wide and variable subject they cannot pretend to be comprehensive; nor can they be used directly for advice on which colour to use in a certain place. For every site has unique characteristics which must be separately studied. The aim is to establish a methodology which can be understood and usefully employed in the field. It must be emphasised however that no amount of methodology can be a substitute for seeing! They only way to study colour is through colour.

The guideline sections are:

- Visual factors
  - Target and background
  - Light
  - Distance
  - Surface
- Colour characteristics
- Colour assessment
  - Environmental impact: colour
  - Questions relating to the background
  - Questions relating to the target
  - Visual objectives
  - Colour options

Colour measurements

Target and background

When we look at any object we see it as a visual 'target' in relation to its immediate surroundings. If it is brighter (more reflective) or more colourful than the surroundings, it is likely to 'catch the eye'. Buildings are seen in a similar way: as incidents which are in greater or lesser contrast with their surroundings. This has been described in terms derived from Gestalt psychology as a *target/background* situation.

Since any object introduced into the environment becomes a visual target in relation to its context, it is necessary to consider the factors determining that relationship. This involves a detailed study of both 'target' and 'background' in terms of the criteria by which colour is determined. These are light, distance and surface, all of which are measurable; and the subjective perceptions of the observer.

Light

The direction and intensity of light and the atmosphere through which it passes controls the light wavelengths falling upon the surfaces of different materials, and thus the colour. Direct sunlight intensifies shadows, emphasising form. But it is important to remember that the more common diffused light reduces shadows, thereby making forms appear as flat shapes which visually coalesce, and seem bulkier.

Distance

The size of any object is relative to the distance from which it is seen. All objects have a scale relationship with their surroundings, which in the countryside is measured in terms of trees, hedges, walls and buildings; in the town largely against buildings. Large new buildings or structures in the landscape will generally be seen in the distance or middle distance; in the town, the view is likely to be close. As the distance increases colours become visually mixed, and finally appear disembodied from the objects. This can be exploited by applying patterns of colour to manipulate form and spatial organisation.

Surface

All surfaces, whether or not they are deliberately coloured, absorb and reflect light. Smooth and shiny surfaces reflect light more directly than rough surfaces, which diffuse it. Absorption depends upon the molecular structure of the material: the colour perceived is determined by the wavelengths not absorbed by the material. Large shiny surfaces should in general be avoided in the landscape because of their eye-catching quality. This applies particularly to buildings with mirror or shiny metallic surfaces, which, even when they are coloured, catch the light and cause glare. At the extreme, it is an effect commonly seen in areas of glass-houses or parked cars. Totally mirror-clad buildings have the exciting potential of water in bringing down the sky, or of reproducing the trees and buildings adjoining. But this is to be enjoyed at close quarters, in the city, where the lightening effect is an asset. The dull mottled surfaces of galvanised electricity pylons and motorway crash barriers blend well with the landscape because their reflective surfaces are broken.

Matching similar colours on different surfaces is difficult. Corrugated materials for example, reflect light and colour differently from plain ones: this also applies to a lesser extent to glossy and matt paint surfaces. Moreover similar, identically coloured surfaces will reflect different colours according to their orientation.

Colour characteristics

Colour has three 'dimensions': hue, value and chroma: they must all be considered. At the landscape distance the light reflective value is the most critical. White, the most reflective 'colour', should, like yellow, be used with restraint for this reason. Although there is a strong traditional precedent in the use of whitewash on farm buildings, they are usually seen in isolation. A number of white 'targets' scattered over a limited area (as occurs with caravans), is visually disruptive. Hues cannot be considered apart from their chromas or intensities. Yellow for example, as its intensity decreases, can be almost as reflective as white, or nearly as dark as black, according to its value. Although yellow is a good landscape colour – occurring in all vegetation, and the majority of natural building materials – in its pure form, it needs to be handled with great care. Large bright areas should almost always be avoided, and its use confined to structural colour or detail.

This applies also to red, which, although generally less reflective than yellow, can make a strong chromatic impact on the landscape. Its presence in vegetation and in many natural building materials, makes it acceptable in the landscape, but most easily in the form of natural ochres and red-browns. Blue, by contrast, is an uncommon landscape colour, which should be used exceptionally rather than habitually. It brings out the worst in grass by relating to the blue content, which makes the bright green of grass so difficult to handle. The characteristic of becoming perceptually brighter when the light is reduced makes it generally an unsuitable colour to relate to vegetation. It should thus be muted or used as a structural or detail colour rather than in large bright areas. There are however instances in which the essential relationship may be with sky or water, or more subtly, with the prevailing light, when it can be used to brilliant effect. In general some degree of contrast is desirable, which is one reason why green is unsuitable as a landscape colour. But the contrast should not be so strident as to inhibit all colour in the surroundings.

Colour assessment

In order to formulate a colour policy it is necessary to make detailed analyses of both target and background; this will be done to greater or lesser degree according to the nature and importance of the project. But it is always essential to visit the site. Large projects in environmentally sensitive areas will need studies made through the seasons, and ideally in different weather conditions. There are several methods of recording colour information. Most people use colour photography for convenience, but the colour is variable. J.P. Lenclos prefers to make sketches with coloured pencils, supplemented by samples of actual materials: rock, soils, building materials, flakes of paint, and specimens of vegetation. This facilitates colour matching in the laboratory. Measurements of reflectivity can be made with a photometer, and colours (that is hues and their chromas) can be matched in the field by different methods using colour swatches.

Environmental impact: colour

For assessment purposes it is useful to compile a questionnaire relating to the type of development and its context, based upon a check-list of items which may be expanded as required to suit the project. For example, the colours of items of detail which may not register in the distant view, will become important at close quarters.

Questions relating to the background

1. What is the extent of the visual field?
2. What is the land-use and settlement pattern? Does it have an identifiable landscape character?
3. What is the predominant colour of the area? What are its constituent colours in terms of rocks, soils, vegetation, traditional and modern buildings and other structures?
4. What colour changes occur?

5. What is the quality of the light? Is the atmosphere, for instance, polluted, habitually damp/clear/changeable?
6. How vulnerable is the area to change? Would it be spoilt/improved, by the addition of a new focus?
7. What colours could appropriately be added?

Questions relating to the target

1. How large an area of the background will it cover?
2. What is the proposed scale/size/form?
3. What materials/textures/colours are proposed?
4. What are the alternatives?
5. What is the aspect? How can the elements be arranged?
6. Do the elements relate to any existing structures? If so how can they be integrated/related?
7. What is the time-scale: for completion/for extension, if any/for the duration of its useful life?
8. How long is the expected life of the surface materials/colours?
9. Are the colours fast? Will the surfaces deteriorate? If so will they be repainted? Will they be cleaned?
10. From where will the building development be seen? How frequently and by how many people will it be seen?
11. Should the development respond to any significant local or regional colour traditions?
12. What are the colour options?

Visual objectives

It is important to decide upon visual objectives at an early planning stage of the development because they will have a strong influence upon the siting, form and materials of the project. The visual objectives are likely to fall within one or more of the following categories:

1. Suppression. Should the whole or part of the building complex be concealed: by burying, earth-mounding, or planting? Should colours be used to reduce impact?
2. Integration. Should the whole or a part of the building complex be integrated by the use of materials and colours which have a particular affinity with the surroundings?
3. Distraction. Should colour be used as a target or series of targets to distract attention away from other parts of the development?
4. Creative expression. Should colour be used as a design element to attract attention to the building or development as a whole?

Colour options

The 'local' surface colours will depend upon the exposed construction materials used in building, on cladding materials, and on applied paint. it is a mistake to try to match the colours of different materials with one another. Some degree of contrast is more effective, and more easily achieved. The choice of materials will limit the choice of colours. In addition, certain colours may be immediately rejected as unsuitable: for example, bright green in the landscape. When these eliminations have been made, a series of colour options should be drawn up, with details of their material, manufacturer and colour reference. Translated into photo-montage, video-montage or model form they can then be used to evaluate the alternatives and find an appropriate solution. It is also useful to erect a large-scale colour panel on site.

Colour measurements

The viewpoints from which the colour measurements will be made must be carefully selected to ensure that they will have a valid relationship with the finished project. In urban or built up areas they should be close, and in the countryside where the structure will be seen in a landscape setting, they will vary from a middle to distant range. At such ranges there is the advantage that the individual textures of plants, and of building materials, visually coalesce, presenting what appear to be abstract areas of colour. It is however often necessary to make a supplementary assessment at close range, as in the case of signs and street furniture which may be sited against a background of buildings or vegetation.

Three factors basically need to be measured: the lightness or reflectivity measured as *value* in the Munsell system, and the *hue* and its intensity or saturation, *chroma* in the Munsell system. The first is important because it is principally on the basis of contrast that we perceive objects in the landscape. Hue and its intensity are clearly important because of the need to select appropriate colours for any new development.

Colour value can be measured by a photometer, or long-range light meter focussed on different parts of the site. Hardy found that the general range of landscape values in all parts of Britain (excluding Northern Ireland) was between Munsell value 4 and value 8, or 12% and 56%, averaged over all seasons under clear and overcast skies. This covered surface geology and bare earth due to agriculture, but excluded such extremes as the dark sides of forest and woodland and bare chalk faces. The value readings for traditional buildings coincided generally with those for surface geology, colour-washed buildings tending to have high values.[1]

Hue and chroma can be measured by direct comparison with colour chips or cards, or through an epidiascope as used by Heath for New Zealand farm buildings.[2] Hardy related these to colour slides for his investigation, but it should be noted that their colour is variable. Lenclos in his French study[3] advocates the use of sketches with crayon which provides a matchable colour.

A relatively simple method of assessing the impact of a structure on the landscape background under particular light conditions is to make a model or more simply a cut-out profile of the structure and arrange it on a stand in front of the view, with or without a surrounding frame. Various models could then be coloured differently and perhaps photographed. Cairns used swatches of alternative colours to relate to photographs taken at different seasons[4].

One of the most comprehensive studies has been undertaken by Professor Hardy of Newcastle University who set up an experiment to assess the colours found in the countryside[5]. Treating it as a 'target and background' situation as described in studies of visual perception, he set out to measure the landscape 'background'. This was done by travelling around England, Scotland and Wales recording the landscape at all seasons, and in clear and overcast light using a Munsell pocket atlas to identify landscape colours. These were then recorded on Agfa CT18 colour slides. As the survey was related to large buildings and their background, the countryside was viewed from a distance at which the individual textures of leaves and plants and their colours had merged into areas of uniform colour. The findings were then described on a Munsell colour circle identifying hues or colours, as 'natural' or 'artificial'. These categories cannot however be considered as precise because of the other variables of *value* and *chroma* which are not recorded in this way. For instance, some hues which occurred at low values and chromas as natural, would appear as artificial had they occurred at high values and chromas. Hardy's main findings were that natural ground surface hues are concentrated in the 10 Red to 10 Green-yellow zones and sky and water in the 10 Blue-green to 10 Purple-blue zone, wtih a small concentration of colour centred in the 5 Red-purple zone due to the presence of heather flowers and certain weeds. The tenth of the Munsell spectrum described as Munsell Green does not occur at all. This provides an illustration both of the limitations of words to describe colours and the folly of choosing 'green' to blend with the landscape.

But pressures are such that it is not often possible to carry out an assessment over a whole year, and it would be of great value if planning and other authorities would undertake comprehensive colour surveys which could be fed into a computer data bank. These could start perhaps with the National Parks, which already have signficant colour character, and be extended over counties and regions, including areas whose pressure for development is greatest. J.P. Lenclos has produced such a study for fifteen *départements* of France[6].

Lenclos' method is based upon a painstaking analysis of all the colour elements on the site: earth, rock, walls, roofs, doors, shutters, windows, together with the impermanent elements including: foliage, moss and lichens. These are then matched with colour cards and assembled in different ways according to a number of stages: firstly of hue, secondly of reflectivity. The colours of roofs and walls are considered with the background as part of the *general palette*, with windows and doors as items of *punctuation*. All are carefully plotted and assembled, and then re-ordered to produce a synthesised recommended palette.

Glossary of terms

Achromatic colours Those without hue: black, white and neutral grey.

Adaptation The adaptation of the eye to differing light conditions. It is the process by which the pupils dilate when one moves from a light to a dark space, and the rods in the retina become active. Conversely the cones become active when the change is from dim to bright light. Adaptation is an essential factor in making colour judgements under different lighting conditions.

Additive colour The mixture of different coloured light beams reflected from a white surface. Red, green and blue lights of equal intensities added together, produce white light; red and green lights produce yellow.

Additive primaries Red, green and blue light, which can be mixed in varying proportions to produce a wide range of different colours.

After image After-images occur when the cones of the retina have become adapted to a particular colour; its complementary colour will appear, even when the eyes are closed.

Brightness The physical term for the intensity of a light source. Sometimes confused with the term *lightness* which refers to the reflectivity or value of surface colours. Also used, ambiguously, to refer to colour saturation.

Chroma The degree of intensity or saturation according to the Munsell System.

Colour Colour can be described objectively in terms of light wavelengths, luminance and purity; or subjectively, in terms of hue, brightness and saturation (for light sources), and hue, lightness and saturation (for surfaces). Hue corresponds to the dominant wavelength, saturation to its 'colourfulness', and lightness to its grey content.

Colour constancy The process by which in our perceptions the colours of objects remain constant under widely varying conditions.

Colour solid A three-dimensional model expressing the three main attributes of colour: hue, lightness and saturation. The vertical axis invariably represents the scale of lightness (value or greyness) from black at the bottom to white at the top, the hues being placed in spectral order around in layers according to their lightness and saturation.

Colour assimilation The overall colour appearance of similar small-scale units such as bricks may be changed by the use of different coloured jointing materials. This process of visual mixing, which increases with distance, is called colour assimilation. This was developed as a technique by the French Impressionist painters and in particular the Pointillists.

Colour attachment The visual attachment of the colour of one surface to another: an object to its background.

Colour system An arrangement of colours according to their attributes which makes colour sampling possible.

Complementary colours Pairs of colours which when mixed as light beams, produce white light. Traditionally blue and yellow, and red and green were considered to be complementary since neither appeared to contain any trace of the other. Each colour produces its complementary after-image.

Fluorescence A brightness additional to that reflected in the normal way due to the absorption of some invisible ultraviolet wavelengths from sunlight which are emitted as additional coloured light.

Hue The attribute by which one colour is distinguished from another.

Intensity Colour saturation. The brightness of a light source.

Iridescence Changing colours due to light interference, refraction and diffraction: seen in soap bubbles and butterflies' wings.

Lightness The 'greyness' of a colour compared with white and black. The degree to which a surface reflects light, described as value in the Munsell System.

Light scattering Light is scattered in all directions by reflection from particles in a transparent medium such as air or water, when the wavelengths approximate to those of the diameter of the particles. Known as Tyndall's scattering after the scientist who first described it, it occurs most commonly with the shorter wavelengths of blue; but also with those of violet and green.

Local colour Artists use the term to describe the 'true colour' of an object seen by average light at fairly close range, as distinct from its appearance under various atmospheric conditions.

Luminescence Light which does not derive directly from an incandescent light source. It

may be due to chemical or electrical processes including fluorescence and phosphorescence.
Optical mixture The process by which coloured light beams or colour patches on a spinning disc, are mixed to combine as different colours.
Pigment Insoluble colouring matter compounds which are especially efficient in selectively absorbing certain light wavelengths and reflecting others.
Primary colours A set of colours from which all other colours can be derived, but no two of which will produce the third. In the additive colour mixing of light, red, green and blue are primary; in subtractive colour mixing, the primaries are magenta, cyan and yellow. Green is usually added to the three pigment primaries, red, yellow and blue, because it is possible to produce a green without traces of either blue or yellow.
Purkinje shift The change from cone to rod vision in response to a reduction in the level of illumination, which makes blues appear more intense and reds darker at twilight. The effect was described by the Czech physiologist J E Purkinje in 1825.
Reflection Reflection describes the light that is neither absorbed nor transmitted, being returned from a surface, and enabling us to see the object. Matt surfaces reflect diffusely, sending the light waves in all directions. Mirror-like surfaces reflect directly, returning the light waves at the same angle. Preferential reflection causes surfaces to appear coloured.
Refraction The bending of light rays as they pass from one medium to another, as for instance from air to water. Shorter wavelengths of light are bent more than that of longer wavelengths, a factor which allows suitably shaped transparent bodies such as prisms to break down white light into a spectrum of colours.
Saturation A term originally used by dyers to describe the strength or vividness of a hue. It is used to describe the intensity and purity of a colour.
Secondary colour A colour such as orange or purple, obtained by mixing two or more primary colours.
Shade A colour obtained by mixing a hue with black.
Simultaneous contrast The apparent differences in contrast between colours that are simultaneously present in the visual field. It is seen in receding ranges of hills which appear to have darker upper edges when contrasted with the lower edges of the adjoining range; or in a grey object which looks lighter against a dark background, and darker against a light background. In colour an adjacent surface may appear tinged with the complementary colour of the background.
Spectral colours The constituent colours of sunlight and white light.
Subtractive colour mixing The process by which colours are subtracted by the superimposition of coloured filters or the addition of dyes or pigments. Yellow, cyan and magenta printing inks absorb almost all the light wavelengths, producing brownish black.
Surface colour Colour that is returned to the eye by reflection from a surface.
Tertiary colour A painter's description for colours produced by mixing two secondary colours.
Tint A colour obtained by a mixing hue with white.
Tone A term used loosely to describe colour modifications; used specifically by Birren to refer to gradation from a hue towards neutral grey.
Value The term used in the Munsell System for lightness of a surface colour. It is roughly but not precisely synomymous with the term greyness used in the BSS Colour Coordination Framework (BS 5252).

Bibliography

Akademie Der Künste *Bruno taut 1880–1938*. Akademie der Künste, Berlin. Ausstellung Katalog 128–1980.
Albers J *Interaction of Colour*, Yale University Press 1971.
Appleton J *The Experience of Landscape*, John Wiley & Sons 1975.
Architect's Journal *Conservation Areas*, Architectural Press, reprint 18th January 1967.
Architect's Journal *Rural Settlement and Landscape*, Architectural Press. 1st January 1976.
Arnheim R *Art and Visual Perception*, Faber 1954.
Ayres J *The Home in Britain*, Shell/Faber & Faber 1981.

Bacon E *Design of Cities*, Thames and Hudson 1967.
Bardi P M *The Tropical Gardens of Burle-Marx*, Architectural Press 1964.
Bartram A *Street Name Lettering in the British Isles*, Lund Humphries 1978.
Beazley E *Designed for Recreation*, Faber 1969.
Birren F *Colour and Human Response*, Van Nostrand Reinhold Co 1969.
Birren F *Principles of Colour*, Van Nostrand Reinhold Co 1969.
Brookes J *Room Outside*, Thames and Hudson 1968.
Brunskill R W *Illustrated Handbook of Vernacular Architecture*, Faber & Faber 1978.
Building Research Station Various Digests on colour and buildings, HMSO

Cairns W J & Ass. + Occidental Oil Co. *Flotta Orkney. Oil Handling Terminal: Visual Impact Appraisal & Landscape Proposals* 1971.
Campbell F J *Current Materials*. Paper delivered at symposium on Colour & the Countryside, March 1982.
Civic Trust *Pride of Place*, Civic Trust 1972.
Colvin B *Land and Landscape*, John Murray 1970.
Clifton-Taylor A *The Pattern of English Building*, Faber & Faber 1980
Clouston B ed *Landscape Design with Plants*, Heinemann 1977.
Cooper G & Sargent D *Painting the Town*, Phaidon 1979.
Countryside Commission *Countryside Conservation Handbook*.
Crowe S *Forestry in the Landscape*, Forestry Commission Bk no 18, HMSO 1966.
Crowe S *The Landscape of Power*, Architectural Press 1958.
Crowe S *Tomorrow's Landscape*, Architectural Press 1956.
Cullen G *Townscape*, Architectural Press 1981.

Design Council *Catalogue of Farm Buildings*, 1977.
Design Council *Colour Finishes for Farm Buildings*, 1975.
Design Council *Design 'In the Countryside'*, no. 287, 1972.
Darley G *The National Trust Book of the Farm*, National Trust/Weidenfeld and Nicholoson 1981.
DOE *Roads and the Environment*, HMSO 1976.
Düttmann, Schmuck, Uhl *Color in Townscape*, Architectural Press 1981.

Evans T & Lycett-Green C *English Cottages*, Weidenfeld and Nicholoson 1982.

Fairbrother N *The Nature of Landscape Design*, Architectural Press 1974.
Faulkner W *Architecture and Color*, Wiley Interscience 1872.
Fowler P *Farms in England*, Royal Commission on Historic Monuments, HMSO 1983.

Gibson J J *The Perception of the Visual World*, Greenwood Press 1974.
Gibson P J *Lichen on Farm Roofs*. Paper delivered at symposium on Colour & the Countryside March 1982.
Gloag H L & Gold M *Colour Co-ordination Handbook*, Building Research Establishment Report. DOE/HMSO 1978.
Gloag H L *Dimensions of Colour Appearance in Architecture*, paper delivered to the Colour Group (GB) May 1977.
Gloag H L *Colour in the Urban Environment*.
Goethe see Matthaei R
Gregory R L *Eye and Brain*, Weidenfeld & Nicholson 1979.
Gregory R L *The Intelligent Eye*, Weidenfeld & Nicholson 1975.
Grigson G *Britain Observed*, Phaidon 1975.

Hackett B *Planting Design*, E & F N Spon 1979.
Hadfield J ed *The Shell Book of English Villages*, Michael Joseph 1980
Hadfield J ed. *The Shell Guide to England*, Michael Joseph 1970
Haigh V *Colour and the Farmed Landscape*. Paper delivered at symposium on Colour & the Countryside, March 1982.
Hardy A C ed. *Colour in Architecture*, Leonard Hill 1967.
Hardy A C *Colour and Farm Buildings*, publ. in Agricultture Nov. 1970.
Hardy A C *Colour Finishes for Static Caravans*, The Caravan Council 1974.
Hardy A C *Colour in the Landscape*, paper presented at the MOT/BRF conference on Roads in the Landscape 1967.
Heath T *Colour for Structures in the Landscape*, Lincoln College, New Zealand 1978.
Hedgecoe J *The Photographer's Handbook*, Ebury Press 1982.
Heron P *The Colour of Colour*, College of Fine Arts, University of Texas 1979.
Hoskins W G *English Landscapes*, BBC Publications 1976.
Hoskins W G *One Man's England*, BBC Publications 1978.
Humphries P H *Castles of Edward the First in Wales*, HMSO 1983.

Itten J *The Art of Color*, Van Norstrand Reinhold Co 1969.

Jekyll G *Colour Schemes for the Flower Garden* (1908), Antique Collectors's Club 1982.

Jekyll G *Wood and Garden* (1899), Macmillan 1982.
Judd D B *A Five-attribute System of describing Visual Appearance*, publ. Amer. Soc. for Testing Matls. Spec. & Tech. no. 298, 1961.

Kemp G van der *A Visit to Giverny*, Kemp 1983.
Klöckner K *Der Fachwerkbau in Hessen*, Callway 1980.
Kueppers H *The Basic Law of Color Theory*, Barrons 1982.
Kunstforum *Farbe und Architektur*, Bd 57 1/83 January.

Lenclos J-P & D *Les Couleurs de la France*, Moniteur 1982.

Maré E de *Colour Photography*, Penguin Books 1968.
Matthaei R ed. *Goethe's Colour Theory* (c. 1800), Studio Vista 1971.
Minnaert M *The Nature of Light & Color in the Open Air*, Dover 1954
Muir R *The English Village*, Thames and Hudson 1981.

Newton E *The Arts of Man*, Thames and Hudson 1960.

Osborne H ed. *The Oxford Companion to Art*, Oxford University Press 1981.

Penoyre J & J *Houses in the Landscape*, Faber & Faber 1978.
Porter T & Mikellaides B *Colour for Architecture*, Studio Vista 1976.
Porter T *Colour Outside*, Architectural Press 1982.
Prizeman J *Your House: the Outside View*, Quiller Press 1982.

Rapoport A *Human Aspects of Urban Form*, Pergamon Press 1977.
Rassmusson S E *Experiencing Architecture*, Chapman & Hall 1964.
Robinson W *The Wild Garden* (1894), Scolar Press 1979.
Rossotti H *Colour: Why the World isn't Grey*, Penguin Books 1983.

Sausmarez M de *Basic Design: the Dynamics of Visual Form*, Studio Vista 1967.
Shepheard P *Gardens*, Design Centre/Macdonald & Co 1969.
Shepheard P *Modern Gardens*, Architectural Press 1953.
Sloane P *Colour: Basic Principles and New Directions*, Studio Vista.
Stokes A *Colour and Form*, Faber & Faber 1937.

Trevor-Roper P *The World through Blunted Sight*, Thames and Hudson 1970.
Tunnard C *Gardens in the Modern Landscape*, Architectural Press (1938) 1948.
Turner T H D *Introduction to 1982 edition Colour Schemes for the Flower Garden* by Gertrude Jekyll.

Varley H ed. *Colour*, Mitchell Beazley 1980.

Weller J *History of the Farmstead*, Faber & Faber 1982.
Weller J *The Role of Colour in Farm Building Design*, paper delivered at symposium on Colour & the Countryside. March 1982.

Notes

Title

The word landscape is used not in the limited sense current in the eighteenth century but in the contemporary sense as referring to all types of open space, both in town and country.

Caption to illustration 1

1 *Isaac Newton is quoted* by H Rossotti in *Colour*. 1983.

Introduction

1 *Colour Constancy* is discussed at length in *Colour* by H Rossotti, *Colour* ed. H Varley, and in papers by H L Gloag.
2 Prizeman J *Your House: the Outside View*, 1980.
3 Hoskins W G *The Making of the Village: The Shell Book of English Villages* ed. J Hadfield 1970.
4 Mumford L *Architecture as a Home for Man* Architectural Record Books. New York 1975.

THE NATURE OF COLOUR

1 Gregory R L *Eye and Brain*, 1979.
2 Wright W D *Colour Vision Characteristics*, publ. Lighting Research & Technology. vol. 7. no. 3.
3–4 Gregory R L *Eye and Brain*, 1979.
5 The effect is known as the Purkinje Shift after the Czech physiologist who described it in 1823. It is well illustrated by viewing pink and blue flowers at midday and in the twilight, as shown in Colour ed. H Varley.
6 Varley H 3d. *Colour*, 1980.
7 Minnaert M *Light and Color in the Open Air*, 1954. Not all authorities are agreed on the precise nature of the atmospheric particles which cause the scattering; Minnaert for example considers them to be of air, while others believe that dust, water vapour and various gases are involved.
8 Minnaert M *Light and Color in the Open Air*, 1954.
9 House J *Monet*, Phaidon 1981.
10 Judd D B *A Five-attribute System of Describing Visual Appearance*, publ. American Society for Testing Materials Specification and Technology, publ. no. 297, quoted by H L Gloag in *Dimensions of Colour Appearance in Architecture*.
11, 12 Kemp G van der A Visit to Giverny, 1983.

Colour Description

1–2 Varley H ed. *Colour*, 1980.
3 Mead Margaret quoted in *Colour Photography* by Eric de Maré, 1968.
4–7 Varley H ed. *Colour*, 1980.
8 Arnheim R *Art and Visual Perception*, 1954.
9 Varley H ed. *Colour*, 1980.
10–11 Gloag H L & Gold M *Colour Co-ordination Handbook*, 1978.

Colour Harmony

1–2 Arnheim R *Art and Visual Perception*, 1954.
3 Hering E, a German physiologist *c.* 1878, quoted by Johannes Itten in *The Art of Color*, 1969.
4 Chevreul M E ed. by Faber Birren 1964. *The Principles of Harmony and Contrast of Colours*, 1879; referred to in *Principles of Color* by Faber Birren, 1969.
5 described by Birren F *Principles of Color*, 1969.
6 Birren F *Principles of Color*, 1969.
7 Moon P & Spencer D E (1944) *Geometric Formulation of Classical Colour Harmony. Aesthetic measure applied to Colour harmony. Area in colour harmony.* J Opt. Soc. Amer. 34 (1, 2 & 3) quoted by H L Gloag in *Colour Coordination Handbook* (1978).
8 Birren F *Principles of Color*, 1969.
9 Arnheim R *Art and Visual Perception*, 1954.

Colour Perception and Association

1 see Introduction note 1; also *Colour Coordination Handbook* by H L Gloag and M Gold, 1978.
2 Gibson J J *The Perception of the Visual World*, 1974.
3 these are the words of R D Thouless from *Phenomenal Regression to the Real Object*, publ. in the British Journal of Psychology no. 21/22, and quoted by Gibson in *The Perception of the Visual World*, They are used to describe the way in which perception seems to deviate from its stimulus in telling us what we know to be there rather than what we see.
4 Itten J *The Art of Color*, 1969
5 Smith P F quotes from a medical paper by Maclean (1964) in *The Dialectics of Colour from Colour for Architecture* by Porter & Mikellaides 1976.
6 Smith P in *Colour for Architecture* by Porter & Mikellaides 1976.

Colour Effects

1 Birren F (1969) *Principles of Color.* Moses Harris was an English printer and entomologist *c.* 1766 who published the first full hue colour chart in *The Natural System of Colours* (reprinted in facsimile with introduction by F Birren 1963). This is illustrated in *Colour* ed. H Varley, 1980.
2 *additive* and *subtractive colour* is illustrated in *Colour* ed. H Varley, 1980.
3 Varley H ed. *Colour*, 1980.
4 Rossotti H *Colour*, 1983.
5 Rossotti illustrates this effect, but the Oxford Companion to Art refers to experiments in the 1940's which suggested that the effect was due rather to brightness or luminance.
6–7 Varley H ed. *Colour*, 1980.
8 Rossotti H *Colour*, 1983.
9 Varley H ed. *Colour*, 1980.
10 Moon P & Spencer D E (1944) quoted by H L Gloag in the *Colour Co-ordination Handbook* (1978).
11 Itten J *The Art of Color*, 1969.
12 *Simultaneous contrast is illustrated in Gloag H L Colour Co-ordination Handbook*, 1978 and Itten J *The Art of Color*, 1969.
13 Goethe J W von English edition of *Goethe's Colour Theory* ed. Matthaei published by Studio Vista. 1971 quoted by J Itten in *The Art of Color*, 1969.
14 Lenclos J P (1982) *Les Couleurs de la France*. Lenclos' method is also referred to in *Colour Outside* by T Porter and the *Colour for Architecture* by Porter & Mikelliades.
15 some examples of 'flicker' or movement are illustrated in *Colour* ed. H Varley and *Colour Outside* by Tom Porter, 1982.
16 a number of examples of 'new' uses of colour on buildings and in the abstract are illustrated in *Colour Outside* by Tom Porter, *Colour for Architecture* by Porter & Mikelliades, *Color in Townscape* by Düttmann, Schmuck and Uhl, Kunstforum International (Bd. 57 1/83) and *Colour* ed. by Varley. *Color in Townscape* for example includes a large area of 'Op Art' paving by Victor Vasarely in the new town of Créteil near Paris.
17 a series of interesting posters has recently been produced by Collet, Dickenson, Pearce and Partners for the Gallagher Tobacco Company using an American computor technique to abstract a naturalistic image into a number of squares of pure hues of different lightness and saturation. Unfortunately, like most advertising, the posters are short-lived.
18 *colour assimilation* is illustrated in *The Colour Co-ordination Handbook* by H L Gloag and M J Gold; also in *The Interaction of Color* by Josef Albers 1975, who calls it the 'von Bezold spreading effect'. The method of optical mixing was used by the French Impressionists.

THE GEOGRAPHY OF COLOUR

The Geography of Colour The title is borrowed from that of an exhibition organised by J-P Lenclos at the Centre Georges-Pompidou in 1977.

Symbolic and Creative Colour

1–4 Sloane P *Colour: Basic Principles and New Directions*.
5 quoted in *Colour Outside* by Tom Porter, 1982.
6 Rassmusson S E *Experiencing Architecture*, 1964.
7 illustrated in *Colour Outside* by Tom Porter, 1982.
8 Stewart C *Gothic Architecture* publ. Longman 1961, quoted by Tom Porter in *Colour Outside*, 1982.

9 Rassmusson S E *Experiencing Architecture*, 1964.
10 Düttmann, Schmuck & Uhl *Color in Townscape*, 1981.
11 Porter T *Colour Outside*, 1982.
12 Lenclos J-P & D *Les Couleurs de la France*, 1982.

Traditional Building in Britain

1 see note 3 in Colour Perceptions
2–3 Clifton-Taylor A *The Pattern of English Building*, 1980.
4 Prizeman J *Your House: The Outside View*, 1980.
5 Klockner K *Der Fachwerkbau in Hessen*, 1980. Nebel H *Sanieren u Modernisieren von Fachwerkbauten*. Grossmann G U *Die Aussenfarbigkeit der Marburger Burgerhauser* publ. Hessische Heimat, March 1983.
6 Pevsner N *The Buildings of England: Shropshire*, quoted by A Clifton-Taylor in *The Pattern of English Building*, 1980.
7 Brunskill R W *Illustrated Handbook of Vernacular Architecture*, 1978.
8 Ayres J *The Home in Britain*, 1981.
9 Prizeman J *Your House: the Outside View*, 1982.
10 information provided by Dr Alex Muirhead of the Suffolk Preservation Society.
11–13 Clifton-Taylor A *The Pattern of English Building*, 1980.
14 Prizeman J (1980) *Your House: the Outside View*, 1982.
15–19 Clifton-Taylor A *The Pattern of English Building*, 1980.

Colour and the Countryside

1–3 Minnaert M *Light and Color in the Open Air*, 1954.
4 Darley G *The National Trust Book of the Farm*, 1981.
5 Hardy A C *Colour in the Landscape*, 1967.
6 Stokes A *Colour and Form* quoted by Christopher Tunnard in *Gardens and the Modern Landscape*, 1948.
7 Goethe J W von quoted by Christopher Tunnard in *Gardens and the Modern Landscape*, 1948.
8 described as texture gradient by J J Gibson *The Perception of the Visual World*, 1984.
9 Minnaert M *Light and Color in the Open Air*, 1954.
10–11 Gibson J J *The Perception of the Visual World*, 1984.
12–13 Minnaert M *Light and Color in the Open Air*, 1954.
14 Porter & Mikellaides *Colour for Architecture*, 1976.
15–16 Minnaert M *Light and Color in the Open Air*, 1954.
17 Crowe S *Forestry in the Landscape*, 1966.

Colour and the Garden

1 Hadfield M A History of British Gardening, 1960.
2 Turner T Introduction and quotations from *Colour Schemes for the Flower Garden* by Gertrude Jekyll (1908), 1982.
3 Colvin B *Land and Landscape*, 1970.
4 Hackett B *Planting Design*, 1979.

Colour in Towns and Cities

1 illustrated in *Colour Outside* by Tom Porter, 1982.
2 Düttmann, Schmuck and Uhl J *Color in Townscape*, 1982. Same examples of Taut's work illustrated in Kunstforum Bd. 57 1/83 January.
3 some of these are illustrated in *Color in Townscape* by Düttmann, Schmuck and Uhl, in *Colour Outside* by Porter, and *Colour for Architecture* by Porter and Mikellaides.
4 Maré E de *A Painter's Eye at Peterlee in Colour in Architecture in Building Materials vol. 26. no. 7. July 1966.*
5 Rassmusson S E *Experiencing Architecture*, 1964.

COLOUR AND NEW STRUCTURES

1 Rassmusson S E *Experiencing Architecture*, 1964.

Colour and the Farm

1–3 Weller J *History of the Farmstead*, 1982.
4 quoted in *The Countryside: a Landscape in Decline* publ. Design no. 287 November 1977.
5 Hardy A C *Colour and Farm Buildings*, publ. in *Agriculture*, November 1970.
6 information on the siting and design of farm buildings is contained in the Design Council's Catalogue of Farm Buildings, structures, components and fittings 1977, and in *Colour and Farm Buildings*, 1975. Also a number of Ministry of Agriculture leaflets deal with the subject.
7–8 Hardy A C *Colour and Farm Buildings*, 1970.
9 BAP *Coloration des Plaques a.c. par sels metalliques*, publ. by Batiments Agricoles et Paysages, 1980.
Caravans
10 Hardy A C *Colour Finishes for Static Caravans* publ. by The Caravan Council, 1974.

Colour and Industry

1 Foster Associates quoted on the use of colour in buildings: *Colour for Architecture* by Porter and Mikellaides, 1976.
2 Rassmusson refers to the work of a German theorist in *Experiencing Architecture*, 1964.
3 see *Colour Outside* by Tom Porter, 1982.

Colour and Power

1 described in consultants report *Flotta Marine Terminal* by W J Cairns and Associates with Occidental Oil and associated companies, 1974.
2 designed by Architects Design Group, now Gordon Graham and Partners.
3 designed by Rex Savidge: described in the Architect's Journal.
4 designed by Gordon Graham and Partners.

Colour and Transport

1 Hardy A C *Colour in the Landscape*, 1967.
2 Hardy A C *Colour in the Landscape*, 1967.
3 information supplied by Tom Turner.
4 DOE *Roads and the Environment*, 1976.
5 Hardy A C *Colour in the Landscape*, 1967.

Colour and Signs

1 information from thesis on lettering by June Lancaster.
2 Beazley E *Designed for Recreation*
3 Worboys Committe for Traffic Signs Regulations and General Directions, 1964.
4 Beazley E *Designed for Recreation*, 1969.

COLOUR GUIDELINES

Colour Measurements

1 Hardy A C *Colour in the Landscape*, 1967.
2 Heath T *Colour for Structures in the Landscape*, 1978.
3 Lenclos J-P *Les Couleurs de la France*, 1982.
4 Cairns W *Flotta Marine Terminal*, 1974.
5 Hardy A C *Colour in the Landscape*, 1967.
6 Lenclos J-P *Les Couleurs de la France*, 1982.